Two-Career Families

HBR WORKING PARENTS SERIES

Tips, stories, and strategies for the job that never ends.

The **HBR Working Parents Series** supports readers as they anticipate challenges, learn how to advocate for themselves more effectively, juggle their impossible schedules, and find fulfillment at home and at work.

From classic issues such as work-life balance and making time for yourself to thorny challenges such as managing an urgent family crisis and the impact of parenting on your career, this series features the practical tips, strategies, and research you need to be—and feel—more effective at home and at work. Whether you're up with a newborn or touring universities with your teen, we've got what you need to make working parenthood work for you.

Books in the series include:

Advice for Working Dads

Advice for Working Moms

Communicate Better with Everyone

Doing It All as a Solo Parent

Getting It All Done

Managing Your Career

Succeeding as a First-Time Parent

Taking Care of Yourself

Two-Career Families

WORKING PARENTS

Tips, stories, and strategies for the job that never ends.

Two-Career Families

**Harvard Business
Review Press
Boston, Massachusetts**

Library of Congress Cataloging-in-Publication Data

Names: Harvard Business Review Press, issuing body.
Title: Two-career families.
Other titles: Two-career families (Harvard Business Review Press) |
    HBR working parents series.
Description: Boston, Massachusetts : Harvard Business Review Press,
    [2022] | Series: HBR working parents series | "Working parents: tips,
    stories, and strategies for the job that never ends."
Identifiers: LCCN 2021036005 (print) | LCCN 2021036006 (ebook) |
    ISBN 9781647822101 (paperback) | ISBN 9781647822118 (ebook)
Subjects: LCSH: Work and family. | Dual-career families. | Work-life
    balance.
Classification: LCC HD4904.25 .T86 2022 (print) | LCC HD4904.25
    (ebook) | DDC 306.3/6--dc23
LC record available at https://lccn.loc.gov/2021036005
LC ebook record available at https://lccn.loc.gov/2021036006
ISBN: 978-1-64782-210-1
eISBN: 978-1-64782-211-8

CONTENTS

Contents

Section 2

Tick Tock
Make Schedules, Goals, and Trade-offs

Contents

Section 5

In Sickness and in Health
Take Care of Each Other

Contents

Epilogue

The Greatest Adventure

INTRODUCTION

Two for the Road

by Daisy Dowling

You're a working parent and so is your partner. You're taking this career-plus-children journey together—as two for the road.

This can bring many wonderful advantages—practical, personal, and even professional. Maybe the fact that you and your partner both work provides you with a sense of security: If one of you loses or changes jobs, or decides to join that risky new entrepreneurial venture, you can still rest easy knowing there's another paycheck to feed the kids on. Maybe it feels great to have a built-in coach and supporter—someone who's equally in the career-and-parenting fray who really "gets it" and *you*—right there at home. Do you relish the fact that your kids have not just one but two working-parent role models? Or maybe you and your partner admire each other's on-the-job accomplishments, and the fact that you're both working now while also being fantastic parents just feels authentic and right.

But I'll venture a respectful guess that it didn't feel quite so right when, after the sitter called in sick last week, the two of you had a spat over who should take over childcare duty that day, when you both faced major deadlines and pressing meetings. It likely didn't leave you with that "we're in this together" feeling when you found yourself bickering over whose new work schedule meant they could handle daycare pickup in the post-pandemic "new normal." I'll bet that pulling your heavy load on the job, combined with childcare, laundry, and homework, often leaves you without enough time for your partner or for yourself. And the tense conversations the two of you have been having about whether or not to pump the career brakes, given the kids' current needs? Those aren't your favorites, either. So yes, of course dual-career family life has upsides, but you're often left wondering how you can *both* succeed at work, be the parents you want to be, remain physically and mentally yourself, *and* keep your partnership prominent, all at the same time.

Let me assure you that both I and my own working-dad husband are right there with you—and that the majority of working parents I coach each year are as well. My husband and I bicker about who-makes-dinner logistics. We talked for hours about whether that big corporate job I was offered would mean too much overall parent time away from the kids. As I write this, I've just coached an ambitious, successful couple delighted to be expecting their second child but worried about what the impending arrival will mean to their work routines and their relationship. To be clear, logistics, disagreements, calendars, job changes, and new babies are only a small part of the issue—visible parts of the iceberg, as it were. The real, underlying matter, which lurks beneath the surface, is the disconcerting lack of any kind of *system* for navigating, deciding, discussing, and succeeding at dual-career working-parent life. There's no one perfect playbook for dual-career working parenthood—but, nevertheless, you still want to approach it with confidence and intent.

Which is precisely what *Two-Career Families* will help you do. Whether you're a hardworking couple considering starting a family (in, let's not forget, a promotion year); two parents in a blended household managing busy client-facing roles while parenting teenagers; LGBTQIA+ partners working on creating a weekly work-plus-family routine that reflects your values and selves; parents of toddlers, and one of you is transitioning back into the workforce after a few years away; or in any other type of dual-career family situation, then this book is for you. In this book you won't find tons of time-saving life hacks or little silver bullets to shoot at the daily stresses of combining career and kids. What you *will* find are habits, conversations, perspectives, and approaches that gently get the two of you onto that same road as working parents, sustainably and long-term. You'll learn new ways of talking about your goals and values, of considering career decisions, of helping each other through periods of work stress, taking good care of yourselves, the kids, and each other—all while handling the challenging bigger picture and the sometimes hazy issues in between.

Because your career, responsibilities, outlook, and family are unique, the way you'll want to use this book will be also. Start by scanning the table of contents. See which chapters and topics grab you, or address what you're living through and thinking about right now, and then dig in. If you're facing a major career transition that involves a geographical move, turn to Rebecca Knight's chapter on just that topic. If you're both exhausted, start with "How Working Parents Can Prioritize Sleep." You may choose to start solo and then share what you've learned with your partner, or decide to go through the book together, issue by issue. Gain ideas, insight, and inspiration on the challenges you're currently facing—and get a head start on ways to tackle situations you anticipate encountering in your careers and lives together.

And be mindful that there is no perfect approach—to this book, to your careers, or to your life. You will hit bumps in the road. But together you will find a way to navigate everything life throws at you, to do what really works and feels right and authentic to you as individuals, as professionals, as a couple, as a family.

Section 1

Go Team!

*Define Your Values and Create
a Shared Vision*

How Dual-Career Couples Make It Work

by Jennifer Petriglieri

Quick Takes

- Communicate about values, boundaries, and fears
- Negotiate roles and divide family commitments
- Support each other through periods of reflection and exploration
- Identify the opportunity in loss
- Address regrets and developmental asymmetries

Camille and Pierre met in their early forties after each one's marriage had ended. Both were deeply committed to their careers and to their new relationship. Camille, an accountant, had felt pressured by her ex-husband to slow her progress toward partnership at her firm. Pierre, a production manager at an automotive company, was embroiled in a bitter divorce from his wife, who had given up her career to accommodate the geographic moves that his required. (As with the other couples I've profiled in this article, these aren't their real names.) Bruised by their past experiences, they agreed to place their careers on an equal footing. Initially things went smoothly, but two years in, Camille began to feel trapped on a professional path that she realized she had chosen because "that was what the smart kids did."

Mindful of their pact, Pierre calmly listened to her doubts and encouraged her to explore alternatives. But as the months wore on, he began to feel weighed down as he juggled providing emotional support to Camille, navigating their complex family logistics (both had children from their former marriages), and succeeding in his demanding job. When he began to question his own career direction, he wondered how the two of them could manage to change course. They couldn't afford to take time out from work, nor could they take much time to reflect and keep their family and relationship afloat. Frustrated and exhausted, both wondered how they could continue to find meaning and fulfillment in their lives.

Dual-earner couples are on the rise. According to Pew Research, in 63% of couples with children in the United States, for example, both partners work (this figure is slightly higher in the EU).[1] Many of these are *dual-career couples*: Both partners are highly educated, work full-time in demanding professional or managerial jobs, and see themselves on an upward path in their roles. For these couples, as for Pierre and Camille, work is a primary source of identity and a primary channel for ambition. Evidence is mounting from sociological research that when both partners dedicate themselves to work and to home life, they reap benefits such as increased economic freedom, a more satisfying relationship, and a lower-than-average chance of divorce.

Because their working lives and personal lives are deeply intertwined, however, dual-career couples face unique challenges. How do they decide whose job to relocate for, when it's OK for one partner to make a risky career change, or who will leave work early to pick up a sick child from school? How can they give family commitments—and each other—their full attention while both of them are working in demanding roles? And when one of them wants to undertake a professional reinvention, what does that mean for the other? They must work out these questions together, in a way that lets both thrive in love and work. If they don't, regrets and imbalances quickly build up, threatening to hinder their careers, dissolve their relationship, or both.

Many of these challenges are well recognized, and I've previously written in HBR about how companies can adapt their talent strategies to account for some of them ("Talent Management and the Dual-Career Couple," May–June 2018). But for the couples themselves, little guidance is available. Most advice treats major career decisions as if one is flying solo, without a partner, children, or aging parents to consider. When it's for couples, it focuses on their relationship, not how that intersects with their professional dreams, or it addresses how to balance particular trade-offs, such as careers versus family, or how to prioritize partners' work travel. What couples need is a more comprehensive approach for managing the moments when commitments and aspirations clash.

My personal experience in a dual-career couple, and my realization that little systematic academic research had been done in this area, prompted a six-year investigation into the lives of more than 100 dual-career couples, resulting in my book, *Couples That Work.*[2] The people I studied come from around the world, range in age from mid-twenties to mid-sixties, and represent a range of professions, from corporate executive to entrepreneur to worker in the nonprofit sector. My research revealed that dual-career couples overcome their challenges by directly addressing deeper psychological and social forces—such as struggles for power and control; personal hopes, fears, and losses; and assumptions and cultural expectations about the roles partners should play in each other's lives and what it means to have a good relationship or career.

I also discovered that three transition points typically occur during dual-career couples' working and love lives, when those forces are particularly strong. It is during these transitions, I found, that some couples craft a way to thrive in love and work, while others are plagued by conflict and regret. By understanding each transition and knowing what questions to ask each other and what traps to avoid, dual-career couples can emerge stronger, fulfilled in their relationships and in their careers. "A Guide to Couple Contracting" can help partners identify, address, and find common ground.

Transition 1: Working as a Couple

When Jamal and Emily met, in their late twenties, trade-offs were the last thing on their minds. They were full of energy, optimistic, and determined to live life to the fullest. Jamal, a project manager in a civil engineering firm, traveled extensively for work and was given increasingly complex projects to lead, while Emily, who worked at a clothing company, had just been promoted to her first management role. They saw each other mostly on weekends, which they often spent on wilderness hiking adventures. They married 18 months after their first date.

Then, in the space of three months, their world changed dramatically. While Emily was pregnant with their first child, Jamal's boss asked him to run a critical infrastructure project in Mexico. Jamal agreed to spend three weeks out of every month in Mexico City; designating some of his pay raise to extra childcare would allow Emily to keep working in Houston, where they lived. But when their daughter, Aisha, was born two weeks early, Jamal was stuck in the Mexico City airport waiting for a flight home. Soon Emily, who was single-handedly managing Aisha, her job, and their home, discovered that the additional childcare wasn't enough; she felt overburdened and unappreciated. Jamal was exhausted by the relentless travel and the stress of the giant new project; he felt isolated, incompetent, and guilty.

After many arguments, they settled on what they hoped was a practical solution: Because Jamal earned more, Emily took a smaller project role that she could manage remotely, and she and Aisha joined him in Mexico. But Emily felt disconnected from her company's head office and was passed over for a promotion, and eventually she grew resentful of the arrangement. By the time Jamal's boss began talking about his next assignment, their fighting had become intense.

A Guide to Couple Contracting

Drawing on my research, I've developed a systematic tool to help dual-career couples who are facing any of the three transitions described in this chapter. I call it *couple contracting,* because to shape their joint path, partners must address three areas—values, boundaries, and fears—and find common ground in each. Values define the direction of your path, boundaries set its borders, and fears reveal the potential cliffs to avoid on either side. Sharing a clear view in these three domains will make it easier to negotiate and overcome the challenges you encounter together.

First, take some time on your own to write down your thoughts about each of the three areas. Then share your reflections with each other. Listen to and acknowledge each other's responses, resisting any temptation to diminish or discount your partner's fears. Next, note where you have common ground and where your values and boundaries diverge. No couple has perfect overlap in those two areas, but if they are too divergent, negotiate a middle ground. If, for example, one of you could tolerate living apart for a period but the other could not, you'll need to shape a boundary that works for both of you.

(continued)

A Guide to Couple Contracting

Values

When our choices and actions align with our values, we feel content; when they don't, we feel stressed and unhappy. Openly discussing your values will make it easier to make choices that align with them. For example, if you and your partner know you both greatly value family time, you'll be clear that neither of you should take a job requiring 70-hour workweeks.

Questions to ask each other:

What makes you happy and proud? What gives you satisfaction? What makes for a good life?

Boundaries

Setting clear boundaries together allows you to make big decisions more easily. Consider three types of boundaries: place, time, and presence.

Questions to ask each other:

Are there places where you'd love to work and live at some point in your life? Are there places you'd prefer to avoid? Understanding that we may sometimes have to put in more hours than we'd like, how much work is too much? How would you feel about our taking jobs in different cities and living apart for a period? For how

---

long? How much work travel is too much, and how will we juggle travel between us?

Fears

Monitoring each other's fears can help you spot trouble and take preventive action before your relationship enters dangerous territory. Many fears are endemic to relationships and careers: You may worry that your partner's family will encroach on your relationship, that over time the two of you will grow apart, that your partner will have an affair, that you will have to sacrifice your career for your partner's, or that you may not be able to have children. But sharing these fears allows you to build greater empathy and support. If you know that your partner is worried about the role of your parents in your lives, for example, you are more likely to manage the boundary between them and your partnership sensitively. Likewise, if you are interested in a risky career transition but worried that financial commitments would prevent it, you might agree to cut back on family spending in order to build a buffer.

Questions to ask each other:

What are your concerns for the future? What's your biggest fear about how our relationship and careers interact? What do you dread might happen in our lives?

The first transition that dual-career couples must navigate often comes as a response to the first major life event they face together—typically a big career opportunity, the arrival of a child, or the merger of families from previous relationships. To adapt, the partners must negotiate how to prioritize their careers and divide family commitments. Doing so in a way that lets them both thrive requires an underlying shift: They must move from having parallel, independent careers and lives to having interdependent ones.

My research shows two common traps for couples negotiating their way through their first transition.

Concentrating exclusively on the practical

In the first transition in particular, couples often look for logistical solutions to their challenges, as Jamal and Emily did when they arranged for extra childcare and negotiated how many weekends Jamal would be home. This focus is understandable—such problems are tangible, and the underlying psychological and social tensions are murky and anxiety provoking—but it prolongs the struggle, because those tensions remain unresolved.

Instead of simply negotiating over calendars and to-do lists, couples must understand, share, and discuss the emotions, values, and fears underlying their decisions. Talking about feelings as well as practicalities can help them mitigate and manage them.

Basing decisions primarily on money

Many couples focus on economic gain as they decide where to live, whose career to prioritize, and who will do the majority of the childcare. But as sensible (and sometimes unavoidable) as this is, it often means that their decisions end up at odds with their other values and desires.

Few people live for financial gain alone. In their careers they are also motivated by continual learning and being given greater responsibilities. Outside work, they want to spend time with their children and pursue personal interests. Couples may be attracted to a location because of proximity to extended family, the quality of life it affords, or their ability to build a strong community. Basing the decision to move to Mexico on Jamal's higher salary meant that he and Emily ignored their other interests, feeding their discontent.

Couples who are successful discuss the foundations and the structure of their joint path forward. First, they must come to some agreement on core aspects of their relationship: their values, boundaries, and fears. Negotiating and finding common ground in these areas helps them navigate difficult decisions because they can agree on criteria in advance. Doing this together is important; couples that make this arrangement work, I found, make choices openly and jointly, rather than implicitly and for each other. The ones I studied who had never addressed their core criteria struggled in later transitions, because those criteria never go away.

Next, couples must discuss how to prioritize their careers and divide family commitments. Striving for 50/50 is not always the best option; neither must one decide to always give the other's career priority.

There are three basic models to consider: (1) In *primary-secondary*, one partner's career takes priority over the other's for the duration of their working lives. The primary person dedicates more time to work and less to the family, and their professional commitments (and geographic requirements) usually come before the secondary person's. (2) In *turn taking*, the partners agree to periodically swap the primary and secondary positions. (3) In *double-primary*, they continually juggle two primary careers.

My research shows that couples can feel fulfilled in their careers and relationships whichever model they pursue, as long as it aligns with their values and they openly discuss and explicitly agree on their options. Couples who pursue the third option are often the most successful, although it's arguably the most difficult, precisely because they are forced to address conflicts most frequently.

To work past their deadlock, Emily and Jamal finally discussed what really mattered to them beyond financial success. They identified pursuit of their chosen careers, proximity to nature, and a stable home for Aisha where they could both actively parent her. They admitted their fears of growing apart, and in response agreed to an important restriction: They would live in the same city and would limit work travel to 25% of their time. They agreed to place their geographic boundaries around North America, and Jamal suggested that they both draw circles on a map around the cities where they felt they could make a home and have two careers. Their conversations and mapping exercise eventually brought them to a resolution—and a new start in Atlanta, where they would pursue a double-primary model. Three years later they are progressing in their careers, happy in their family life, and expecting a second child.

Transition 2: Reinventing Themselves

Psychological theory holds that early in life many people follow career and personal paths that conform to the expectations of their parents, friends, peers, and society, whereas in their middle years many feel a pressing need for *individuation*, or breaking free of those expectations to become authors of their own lives. This tends to happen in people's forties, regardless of their relationship status, and is part of a process colloquially known as the midlife crisis.

We tend to think of a midlife crisis mostly in personal terms (a husband leaves his wife, for example, and buys a sports car), but in dual-career couples, the intense focus on professional success means that the partners' job tracks come under scrutiny as well. This combined personal and professional crisis forms the basis of the second transition. Camille and Pierre, whose story began this article, were in the midst of it.

As each partner wrestles with self-redefinition, the two often bump up against long-settled arrangements they have made and the identities, relationship, and careers they have crafted together. Some of those arrangements— whose career takes precedence, for example—may need to be reconsidered to allow one partner to quit a job and explore alternatives. It may be painful to question the choices they made together during the previous transition and have since built their lives around. This can be threatening to a relationship; it's not uncommon for one partner to interpret the other's desire to rethink past career choices as an inclination to rethink the relationship as well, or even to potentially end it. Couples who handle this transition well find ways to connect with and support each other through what can feel like a very solitary process.

The second transition often begins—as it did for Camille and Pierre—when one partner reexamines a career or life path. That person must reflect on questions such as: What led me to this impasse? Why did I make the choices I made? Who am I? What do I desire from life? Whom do I want to become? They should also take time to explore alternative paths, through networking events, job shadowing, secondments, volunteer work, and so forth. Such individual reflection and exploration can lead couples to the first trap of the second transition.

Mistrust and defensiveness

Living with a partner who is absorbed in exploring new paths can feel threatening. Painful questions surface: Why is my partner not satisfied? Is this a career problem or a relationship problem? Am I to blame? Why do they need new people? Am I no longer enough? These doubts can lead to mistrust and defensiveness, which may push the exploring partner to withdraw further from the relationship, making the other even more mistrustful and defensive, until eventually the relationship itself becomes an obstacle to individuation, rather than a space for it.

In such a situation, people should first be open about their concerns and let their partners reassure them that the angst is not about them or the relationship. Next, they should adopt what literary critics call *suspension of disbelief*—that is, faith that the things they have doubts about will unfold in interesting ways and are worth paying attention to. This attitude will both enrich their own lives and make their partners' exploration easier.

Finally, they should understand their role as supporters. Psychologists call this role in a relationship the *secure base* and see it as vital to the other partner's growth.

Originally identified and described by the psychologist John Bowlby, the secure base allows us to stretch ourselves by stepping outside our comfort zone while someone by our side soothes our anxieties about doing so. Without overly interfering, supporters should encourage their partners' exploration and reflection, even if it means moving away from the comfortable relationship they've already established.

Being a secure base for a partner presents its own trap, however.

Asymmetric support

In some couples one partner consistently supports the other without receiving support in return. That's what happened to Camille and Pierre. Pierre's experience in his former marriage, in which his wife gave up her career for his, made him determined to support Camille, and he initially stepped up to be a secure base for her. Their lives were so packed, however, that Camille had trouble finding the energy to return the favor. The result was that her exploration and reflection became an impediment to Pierre's, creating a developmental and relationship deadlock. It is important to remember that acting as a secure base does not mean annihilating your own wishes, atoning for past selfishness, or being perfect. You can be a wonderful supporter for your partner while requesting support in return and taking time for yourself. In fact, that will most likely make you a far better (and less resentful) supporter.

In my research I found that couples who make it through their second transition are those in which the partners encourage each other to do this work—even if it means that one of them is exploring and providing support at the same time.

Once the exploring partner has had a chance to determine what they want in a career, a life, or a relationship, the next step is to make it happen—as a couple. Couples need to renegotiate the roles they play in each other's lives. Take Matthew and James, another pair I spoke with, who had risen through the professional ranks in their 18 years together. When Matthew realized that he wanted to get off what he called the success train—on which he felt like a mere passenger—both he and James had to let go of their identity as a power couple and revisit the career-prioritization agreement they had forged during their first transition. Initially Matthew was reluctant to talk to James about his doubts, because he questioned whether James would still love him if he changed direction. When they started discussing this, however, they realized that their identity as a power couple had trapped them in a dynamic in which both needed to succeed but neither could outshine the other. Acknowledging and renegotiating this unspoken arrangement allowed James to shoot for his first senior executive position and Matthew to transition into the nonprofit sector. The time and care they took to answer their existential questions and renegotiate the roles they played in each other's lives set them up for a renewed period of growth in their careers and in their relationship.

Transition 3: Loss and Opportunity

Attending her mother's funeral was one of the most difficult experiences of Norah's life. It was the culmination of two years of immense change for her and her husband, Jeremy, who were in their late fifties. The change began when their fathers unexpectedly passed away within five weeks of each other, and they became caregivers for Norah's ailing mother just as their children were leaving the nest and their own careers were in flux.

Jeremy is a digital visual artist. His studio's main projects were ending because a big client was moving on. Though he was sad, he had become confident enough to feel excited about whatever might come next. Norah had been working for the same small agricultural machinery business for 26 years; she had once wanted to change careers but felt that she couldn't do so while Jeremy was relying on her for emotional and logistical support. Now she was being asked to take an early retirement deal. She felt thrown on the scrap heap despite her long commitment to the company. No career, no parents, no children to care for—who was she now? She felt disoriented and adrift.

The third transition is typically triggered by shifting roles later in life, which often create a profound sense of loss. Careers plateau or decline; bodies are no longer what they once were; children, if there are any, leave home. Sometimes one partner's career is going strong while the other's begins to ebb. Having raced through decades of career growth and child-rearing, couples wake up with someone who may have changed since the time they fell in love. They may both feel that way. These changes again raise fundamental questions of identity: Who am I now? Who do I want to be for the rest of my life?

Although loss usually triggers it, the third transition heralds opportunity. Chances for late-in-life reinvention abound, especially in today's world. Life expectancy is rising across the globe, and older couples may have several decades of reasonably good health and freedom from intensive parenting responsibilities. As careers and work become more flexible, especially for those with experience, people can engage in multiple activities more easily than previous generations could—combining advisory or consulting work with board service, for example. Their activities often include giving back to the community, leaving some kind of legacy, mentoring younger generations, rediscovering passions of their youth, or dedicating themselves more to friendships.

Their task in the third transition is to again reinvent themselves—this time in a way that is both grounded in past accomplishments and optimistic about possibilities for the future. They must mourn the old, welcome the new, figure out how the two fit together, and adjust their life path to support who they want to become.

One thing that struck me when I spoke to couples in their third transition is that it's most powerful when partners reinvent themselves together—not just reflecting jointly, as in the other transitions, but actually taking on a new activity or project side by side. When one is curious about a partner's life and work as well as one's own, an immense capacity for mutual revitalization is unlocked. I met many couples who were charting new paths out of this transition that involved a merging of their work—launching a new business together, for example.

The third transition also has its traps.

Unfinished business

For better or for worse, earlier relational patterns, approaches, decisions, and assumptions will influence how a couple's third transition unfolds. I found that the most common challenge in managing this transition was overcoming regret about perceived failures in the way the partners had "worked" as a couple—how they had prioritized their careers, or how each partner had supported the other's development (or not).

To move through the third transition, couples must acknowledge how they got where they are and commit to playing new roles for each other in the future. For example, Norah and Jeremy had become stuck in a pattern in which Norah was Jeremy's supporter. By recognizing this—and both their roles in cementing it—they were able to become more mutually supportive.

Narrow horizons

By the time a couple reaches the third transition, they will probably have suffered their fair share of disappointments and setbacks. They may be tired from years of taking care of others, or just from staying on the treadmill. As their roles shift and doubts about their identities grow, reinvention may be beyond consideration. In addition, because previous generations retired earlier, didn't live as long, and didn't have access to the gig economy, many couples lack role models for what reinvention can look like at this stage of life. If they don't deliberately broaden their horizons, they miss opportunities to discover themselves anew.

So couples must explore again. Even more than in the second transition, they need to flirt with multiple possibilities. Like healthy children, who are curious about the world, themselves, and those around them, they can actively seek new experiences and experiment, avoid taking things for granted, and constantly ask "Why?" Most of us suppress our childhood curiosity as life progresses and responsibilities pile up. But it is vital to overcome the fear of leaving behind a cherished self and allow ambitions and priorities to diversify. Exploring at this stage is rejuvenating.

Shifts in people's roles and identities offer a perfect excuse to question their current work, life, and loves. Many people associate exploring with looking for new options, which is surely important. But it's also about questioning assumptions and approaches and asking, "Is this really how things need to be?"

Having rebalanced their support for each other, Norah and Jeremy could open up to new possibilities. Having earned financial security from their previous work, they sought reinvention not only in their careers but also in their wider roles in the world. Encouraging each other, they both transitioned to portfolio working lives. Jeremy became a freelance digital visual artist, took a part-time role teaching young art students at a local college, and dedicated more time to his passion of dinghy sailing. Norah retrained to be a counselor working with distressed families and began volunteering at a local agricultural museum. With these new opportunities and more time for each other and their friends, they felt newfound satisfaction with their work and with their relationship.

Conclusion

The challenges couples face at each transition are different but linked. In their first transition, the partners accommodate to a major life event by negotiating the roles they will play in each other's lives. Over time those roles become constraining and spark the restlessness and questioning that lead to the second transition. To successfully navigate the third transition, couples must address regrets and developmental asymmetries left over from their first two transitions.

No one right path or solution exists for meeting these challenges. Although the 50/50 marriage—in which housework and childcare are divided equally between the partners, and their careers are perfectly synced—may seem like a noble ideal, my research suggests that instead of obsessively trying to maintain an even "score," dual-career couples are better off being relentlessly curious, communicative, and proactive in making choices about combining their lives.

Adapted from an article in Harvard Business Review, *September–October 2019 (product #R1905B).*

2

Understanding and Communicating Your Core Values as a Working Parent

by Stewart D. Friedman and Alyssa F. Westring

Quick Takes

- Identify your values to help you make decisions, both large and small
- Consider the events in your life that helped shape who you are
- Write down five core values and what they mean to you
- Reflect and revise as necessary
- Ask your partner to write down their core values
- Discuss your individual and shared values together

A fundamental aspect of becoming an effective leader is understanding and then communicating your core values. Leaders who are aware of their values, convey them clearly, and act in alignment with them are engaged, generate high performance, and inspire commitment.[1] It pays to value values.

Working parents, who face a significant leadership challenge in raising children, can benefit from value-driven leadership. Often overwhelmed by the struggle to make smart decisions about when, where, and how to invest our attention, not many of us working parents stop and reflect on our values. Instead, we tend to internalize the values of our society and people around us, usually unconsciously. Social media amplifies the impact of social comparisons, making it harder to stay centered, to know ourselves. When we lack a clear set of values, or fail to communicate them, we're rudderless and have no guiding compass.

When we identify and express our values, we can more readily use what we truly care about as the basis for making decisions, large and small. In our research, we've found that people who bring a well-articulated set of core values to all parts of life experience less stress, greater harmony, and better performance at home, in their communities, and for themselves personally.

To spur your thinking as you consider your own values—those you aspire to embody in your career, as a parent, and in the rest of your life—here are a few examples listed by working parents in our research on the application of leadership principles to the art of parenting:

Achievement: A sense of accomplishment or mastery, striving to be the best

Adventure: New and challenging opportunities, excitement, risk

Collaboration: Close, cooperative working relationships, being part of a team

Courage: A willingness to stand up for your beliefs and do the difficult thing—despite any fears

Generosity: Being one who gives

Humor: The ability to laugh at yourself and at life

Love: That indescribable feeling when your kids run up to give you a hug after work

Responsibility: Doing what you say you will do

Spirituality: Believing there is something greater than human beings

Remember that values are relatively stable over time and rather broad, not tied to specific people, places, and times. They are usually influenced by significant events in your life history.[2]

If you've not ever done so, start by thinking about what matters most to you, and why. Try to come up with about five values and write them down (see sidebar "Identify Your Values"). Don't limit yourself to the examples we listed. If you're stuck, do an online search for a list of values and pick those that most accurately represent you, and then think about why, with reference to the road you've traveled so far. Of course, you can always revise, so allow yourself to be as candid as possible.

The next step is communicating those values to the people who matter most to you. Start with your partner(s) in parenting—those with whom you're raising children. This could be a spouse, but it could also be an ex-spouse, a close relative, a life partner, or a dear friend. It's useful to ask them to do this exercise on their own and to then talk over your distinctive and your common values. Just as leaders in groups and organizations need to establish shared values, parenting partners too must identify the values that inform their lives.

Take Emma and Marcos Lopez, from Houston, Texas, who participated in our Parents Who Lead workshop. Emma is a management consultant, and Marcos, a former captain in the army, is an investment manager.

Identify Your Values

On your own, take 30 minutes or so to think about your values, what matters most to you, and why. Come up with about five values. Write them down, then take a break. After at least an hour, come back and fiddle with them, revising each one as needed. Don't limit yourself to the examples we listed; do an online search for a list of values and select those that best represent you. It can help to reflect on significant experiences in your life and how those episodes determined what you care about most deeply (such as Emma's childhood memory of her father's job loss).

The values you list should be relatively stable over time and rather broad, not tied to specific people, places, and times. This is a living list—you can always revise. Take your time to find the right words, images, or stories to help you identify your core values—what they really mean to you and why they're important. Take some time for reflection.

Share this exercise with your partner(s) in parenting and ask them to come up with their own list of core values and definitions. Use these lists as a starting point to have a conversation about where your individual and family values overlap—and where they expand. Different people can have different ideas about what a value means, so capturing definitions independently before

(continued)

Identify Your Values

discussing them together will help ensure that when you're identifying your family's core values that you're speaking the same language.

Sample core values: achievement, adventure, collaboration, courage, generosity, humor, love, responsibility, spirituality

My Core Values

List your values and then take some time to write your own definition of the value, share an image it conjures for you, or draft a brief story that illustrates how this value grounds you. You may draft more than one round

TABLE 2-1

My core values

My core values	Why they matter to me
1.	
2.	
3.	
4.	
5.	

Adapted from "Identify Your Values," in *Parents Who Lead,* by Steward D. Friedman and Alyssa F. Westring, p. 28.

---

as you think through the values and why they matter. Once you have a solid list of values and notes about their importance to you, ask your parenting partner(s) to do the same independent activity. Once they also have a solid list, share them with each other.[1]

Comparing and Sharing Core Values

It may be useful to list your five core values beside those of your partner(s). Discussing the lists together can help launch a wider discussion with your children about your family's shared values.

TABLE 2-2

Our core values

My core values	My parenting partner's core values*	My parenting partner's core values	Our family's core values
1.			
2.			
3.			
4.			
5.			

*Add columns as necessary to make room for all partners to record their core values.

Adapted from "Identify Your Values," in *Parents Who Lead*, by Steward D. Friedman and Alyssa F. Westring, p. 28.

They have a 4-year-old and a 7-year-old. They both listed "career success" as a core value.

But this confused them because they sensed that they held quite different attitudes about their work. Looking more deeply, it turned out that career success meant something different to each of them. Emma remembered a period of her adolescence during which her family struggled to make ends meet after her father was laid off. She realized that the intense stress her family experienced then played a significant role in forming who she became. That's why, for Emma, career success primarily means having sufficient funds stashed away and enough transferable job skills so she does not have to worry about economic security.

For Marcos, a veteran who embraced the clear hierarchy in the military ranking system, career success meant achieving promotions and seniority. Certainly Marcos, like Emma, cares about economic security, but he does not equate it with success. Similarly, Emma cares about recognition, but it is not paramount when she thinks of what success means.

Articulating these distinctions helped them better understand the way they each approach their careers. And when it came to thinking about what they wanted for their future, they were able to envision how they could support each other more carefully and compassionately, not only in their respective careers but also in their roles as mother and father to their kids.

Most people assume their partners know each other's values. Yet even people who enjoy close long-term relationships are often surprised when they reveal their core values to each other. Indeed, research has shown that we're not nearly as accurate as we think when it comes to judging the values, experiences, and goals of those closest to us.[3] You might be surprised by what you find when you share your deepest-held values.

For Emma and Marcos, discussing their values shed new light on one another, despite the fact that they've known each other for 12 years. Marcos would often get frustrated by Emma's always-on, 24/7 availability for her consulting work. He'd frequently find her lit by the glow of her laptop in bed after he assumed she was turning in for the night. It was only after learning more about this aspect of Emma's family history and the traces it left that both he and Emma came to understand that her work ethic was driven, at least in part, by worries about losing her economic security and a fear that she wouldn't get placed on future consulting projects if she didn't perform at a high level on the current one.

For Emma and Marcos, clarifying and communicating their values was an essential first step in becoming values-driven leaders in all parts of their lives. From there, they were able to create a vision for the future that incorporated both of their definitions of career success and other shared and unique values they identified. They were able to strengthen their bonds with the people who matter most to them by communicating these values and to experiment with a few innovations in how they enact their values in their daily lives.

Identifying and describing your core values to our partners in parenting, and being genuinely curious about what they mean, is a crucial part of becoming a parent who leads. Your values are the basis for making mindful choices in both the everyday and the momentous decisions we face. And the foundation on which your children stand is strengthened when you take to heart the leadership challenge of striving to act in a way that's in accord with what you care about most.

Adapted from "How Working Parents Can Regain Control Over Their Lives," on hbr.org, March 5, 2020 (product #H05GJ6).

Dual-Career Couples and Identity

by Erin Reid

Quick Takes

Forget "breadwinner"; a modern identity of "breadsharer" is emerging for men in heterosexual partnerships.

- Breadsharers value each partner's right to pursue their professional and personal goals

- Breadwinners view their wives' careers as having little value, even when their spouse's salary is higher than their own

- Men's careers are shaped by their interpretation of the status and value of their wives' careers

- Breadsharers are open to possibilities for their own careers outside the pathway their firms had set for them

P rofessional careers are notorious for demanding that people be single-mindedly devoted to work. It's a demand that is often especially acute for men, who face rigid expectations that being a successful man requires having a successful career, and that "success" means power and money. While some men fall back on the classic identity of a breadwinner (whose spouse places his career first or does not work), others respond to this tension by adopting the modern identity of what I call a "breadsharer."[1] My research reveals how men's evaluations of the prestige and social worth of their wives' work shaped how they positioned their wives' earnings—namely in ways that diminished or elevated their financial value.

These different interpretations of the social status and financial value of their wives' careers provided men with different ways of approaching their own careers. Breadsharers sought to remain professionally flexible to maximize their ability to respond to their wives' career opportunities and were uncommitted to any particular pathway and open to leaving their organization. Bread-winners, however, seeing no need to be flexible around their wife's career, tended to be more committed to achieving success within their organization's hierarchy.

About the Research

I studied men working at a global strategy consulting firm. As in many such firms, the consultants I studied were expected to be primarily devoted to their work: to be willing to travel far from family and work long days and weekends with very little notice. I interviewed 42 hetero-sexual married men at the firm. These men ranged in age from their mid-twenties to their early sixties and were employed at different levels of the firm's hierarchy.

Men at this firm generally believed that to be success-ful, they had to be fully devoted to their employer and willing to prioritize their work over any work a wife did. As evidence of this equation, they pointed to senior men at the firm, who were almost all married to women who did not work outside the home. But this was not true of the men in my sample. When I began this research, I was told by an insider that most men at the firm had stay-at-home wives. In my sample of 42 married men, 23 of their wives worked full-time and 13 worked part-time. Just six of the 42 wives were not working at the time of the in-terview. There was thus a clear tension in the firm be-tween common beliefs about men's family lives and the actual characteristics of men's families. Among the men I interviewed, this tension led to a fair amount of career angst—and some marital conflict.

Breadsharers

Some men (23 of them, 60% of the sample) conceived of themselves as breadsharers—husbands who valued enabling each partner to pursue their work and family goals. These men described their wives' work in glowing terms, regarding it as high status and worthy of respect. They spoke at length of how important their wives' work was, how well it was regarded by others, and of their wives' many career accomplishments. For example, one man described his wife in the following way:

> [Her] skills make her stand out in a sea of experts.
> . . . She's an excellent public speaker. And one of
> her gifts is that she's able to convey very complex
> concepts to lay audiences and expert audiences. . . .
> Whenever she speaks at any conference, she's like,
> nine times out of 10, she's the top-rated speaker on
> the evaluation forms.

These men used language that elevated the value of their wives' earnings. One man described his wife as his "gravy train." Another explained in detail why his wife's earnings were more important than their dollar value might suggest: "The fact that she doesn't work full-time is probably what makes us at odds. But otherwise, on a per-day wage, we probably make the same money. . . . We both do feel quite empowered at our work, because the other works." Describing a difficult situation at work, he explained that his wife's earnings had empowered him to stand up for himself because, "I knew, right, there was no need to [worry about being fired]. It's not like we were going to go hungry or anything—you know, the mortgage will be paid."

Valuing their wives' work so highly, these men positioned themselves in sharing terms: placing importance on both partners being able to pursue their work and family-related desires, hopes, and dreams. They supported their wives' work alongside—and sometimes ahead of—their own. One explained: "I want to make sure she continues to be in a professional situation where she can [succeed], and that, in turn, you know, puts pressure back on me to sort of say, 'OK, wait. Our life is not going to be the one where I get to do whatever the [expletive] I want job-wise, just because my life is not the center.'"

This support for their wives' careers meant that men were uncertain about the direction of their own careers. The firm demanded an unwavering attention to work, which would lead to a pathway to partnership. But these men felt that their wives' careers required that they themselves remain adaptable and open to changing jobs, cities, or countries. These men were thus not so committed to continuing along the pathway the firm expected of them.

They were aware that, in this, their own expectations for themselves differed from the expectations they faced at the firm. One told me, "We're an interesting couple in that I went to business school, I work as a consultant in the professional services space, in a world where in many ways many of the men in the consulting world, right, are the primary breadwinners in the family and I am not that."

Breadwinners

A smaller group of men (17 of them, 40% of the sample) positioned themselves in terms consistent with the traditional male breadwinner identity. These men accorded low social status to their wives' work, which seemed to prime them to view this work as having little financial importance to the family. This happened even when wives seemed—to an external observer—to be quite financially successful.

One minimized his wife's career achievements, saying, "She could have done much more than she has [in her field], but she chose a different path. What I call, you know—being a project manager in the home is the way I describe it . . ." His wife contributed one-third of the family's income—about a six-figure salary.

Another framed his wife's (considerable) wages in ways that seemed to make them disappear: "I said to her, 'If you take your job and net out all of the daycare expenses and net out all of the extra tax that we have to pay because you work, we'd fundamentally be making the same amount of money between us.'" These men's characterizations of their wives' earnings as fundamentally unimportant, somewhat frivolous, and optional echo a long-standing cultural history of the value of women's work being diminished through labels such as "pin money."

Having diminished the status and financial value of their wives' work, these men easily laid claim to the identity of a work-devoted breadwinner, which they viewed as essential to their potential career success. One man (whose wife was a full-time professional in a similar role and earned more than he did) put it this way: "Work-life balance is less of an option for the guy if he feels the need to be successful and provide for the family. And I guess that's the situation that I'm in right now."

These men, unlike the breadsharers, mostly intended to stay at the firm and make partner. And why wouldn't they? They had made sense of their wives' careers in ways that freed them to devote themselves to their work as their firm demanded. Yet while some seemed quite happy to be breadwinners, others felt trapped: Even though they claimed a breadwinner identity, it was not always a completely satisfying one.

• • •

Why should we care about how men identify themselves in relation to their wives' careers? We often focus on how women's work lives are shaped by their family lives, but the ways that men's work lives are shaped by *their* family circumstances are too often ignored. This study showed that how men in professional careers defined themselves in relation to their work, as well as how they approached their careers, was very much shaped by how they interpreted the social status and financial value of their wives' work.

The importance of status in men's interpretations was somewhat unexpected; in our conversations about work, career, and couples, we often focus on earnings and work hours. This research shows that social status—worth, esteem, and respect—matters too for couples' careers. No husband with a wife who was a doctor or lawyer minimized her career or discounted her earnings, no matter how much or little she worked or earned.

Finally, this work shows that money matters in couples' careers, but not in the ways we think. Salaries are more than dollars and cents; they have a social meaning, and that meaning is quite malleable.

Adapted from "Whether a Husband Identifies as a Breadwinner Depends on Whether He Respects His Wife's Career—Not on How Much She Earns," on hbr.org, August 15, 2018 (product #H04HSH).

Section 2

Tick Tock

*Make Schedules, Goals,
and Trade-offs*

Finding Balance as a Dual-Career Couple

by Amy Jen Su

Quick Takes

- Adopt a team name to reinforce your "in it together" mindset

- Say no to things where you don't add unique value

- Divvy up responsibilities according to strengths and interests

- Schedule regular look-ahead meetings to plan and set expectations

W hen both you and your partner have busy, demanding careers, reaping the benefits of being a dual-career couple and showing up as your best self in every realm of your life is a challenge. Negotiating whose career takes prominence at any given time, juggling two work schedules and household and family duties (including caring for aging parents), and maintaining healthy boundaries between work and the rest of your life are often the most difficult areas to navigate. In my role as an executive coach, it's becoming increasingly common for my clients to seek advice concerning not just their career goals but strategies for helping them succeed in other parts of their lives. While each household is different, the couples I've seen overcome these challenges have developed systems that optimize their time and energy—as a unit. Here are some of the most successful practices my clients have adopted.

Think of Your Family as a Team

When you have a demanding career, it's easy to become so wrapped up in your work that your time at home gets shuffled down the priority list. To overcome this, you need to give your family or partner the same level of dedication that you give to your team at work.

Coming up with a name for your home team—or your family—is a fun way to shift your mindset. Doing so can help remind you and your partner that it should never be "my career versus your career." Rather, view yourselves as allies. One leader I worked with and his wife—who also had a successful career—chose the name "Team Quinn" after their family surname. Another couple picked the acronym GBG, which stood for "Go Bernsteins Go!"

These names helped them see each other more fully as partners navigating day-to-day challenges, just as they do with their colleagues at work. Team Quinn began planning a home schedule as a unit—accounting for career demands, kid activities, and fun family outings. In doing so, they were able to reduce the resentments that often arise when dual-career couples fail to work together.

Get Comfortable Saying "No"

As your and your partner's careers advance, you may gain more influence and receive an increasing number of requests beyond your day-to-day work responsibilities. You may be invited to attend client dinners, join boards, speak at events, or even become mentors. These activities are often rewarding, but they require time and energy. To maintain a healthy work-life equation, you'll need to get comfortable saying no. But knowing when to turn down a request isn't always easy.

One professional I worked with felt an obligation to join her son's school board because she wanted to be involved in supporting his education, and many of her colleagues had done the same for their children. But the more we explored the issue, the more it became clear that taking on this role was more of a "should" than a "want to." Ultimately, it would tip the scales of what was already a tight situation at home.

My client considered the value-add of her options. She could spend her time outside of work with the parents and teachers on the board, or she could use it for quality time with her son. She and her spouse chose the latter. By having an honest conversation about what was important to them, they were able to shift around their schedules and show up for their son in a way that worked best for the entire family.

To find the work-life equation that supports your best self, you'll need to do the same. Carefully consider the cost-benefit of each request you receive by asking yourself the following questions:

- Is it something for which you can uniquely add value?

- Will you derive value by attending or joining?

- What would be the impact on your spouse and home team?

You are painfully aware that you can't do it all—and neither can your partner. That's why every request you accept should have a significant value-add.

Play to Each Other's Strengths and Interests

Staying on top of household and family responsibilities is a continuous struggle. You have to be strategic and disciplined about who does what, especially as your work and family roles grow.

Divvying up responsibilities according to each other's strengths and interests can be a lifesaver. One couple I consulted were in constant conflict due to the stresses of juggling household duties. To ease the tension, I had them make a list of their responsibilities—everything from unloading the dishwasher to managing bills to getting their kids to and from extracurriculars. Next, I asked them to categorize each item on the list as "loathe," "don't mind," or "enjoy." The couple was then able to reassign items based on each person's strengths and interest levels, dramatically decreasing tension and maximizing their capacity to be effective and present. If you find that a few items on your own list are important but loathsome to both you and your partner, outsourcing can be a tremendously helpful option, if you have the means.

Schedule Regular "Look-Ahead" Meetings

As part of a shared life, you and your partner will have to do some planning to negotiate expectations and make decisions about whose career takes the front seat. To do this, dual-career couples need to be in constant communication. A simple solution is to schedule regular look-ahead meetings to plan and set expectations. These meetings are times for open, honest communication, which will help you both stay actively involved in big decisions about career changes, projects, or goals.

Below are a few time frames to follow. Use the ones that work best for you and your partner:

- **Annually:** Once a year, look ahead and block off vacations, school performances, conferences, and other important events you know are coming up.

- **Quarterly/Monthly:** Once a month, plan for upcoming travel, deadlines, or busy work periods.

- **Weekly:** Once a week, discuss your plan for the days ahead to minimize surprises and frustrations.

One of my clients found that a weekly look-ahead meeting was critical for him and his spouse to stay coordinated. Every Sunday morning at breakfast, they pull out their laptops to do a quick scan of the week: who is doing what and who is going where. This helps them stay in sync and share important updates, and it has become a much-anticipated form of quality time.

In addition to keeping you and your partner on the same page, look-aheads are great times to ask each other for support. If you have a critical presentation and need more time to work on it, or if your partner is anticipating an especially busy week, a look-ahead allows you both to plan and prepare. When the unexpected arises, as it inevitably will, you'll already know what's on tap for each other. As a result, you'll be able to more easily pivot and support the spouse who's in crunch time.

Create Clear "Time Zones" for Work and Family Time

With a greater shift to working at home, maintaining clear boundaries between what is work time and what is family time is not easy. It can be difficult to fight the urge to pick up the laptop or have one more work video meeting as it bumps up closely to dinner time. One way to break this cycle is to create clear "time zones."

Time zones are blocks of productive work time. They can also be used to denote when you and your partner will discuss work, rather than letting it leak into every conversation. For example, one professional I coached added the following time zones to her and her spouse's Saturday schedule:

- 9 to 10 a.m.: Have breakfast together, be fully present

- 10 to noon: One partner catches up on work (time zone #1)

- 1 to 3 p.m.: The other partner catches up on work (time zone #2)

- 3 p.m.: Have fun with friends or family for the rest of the day

Setting time zones can also help clarify your availability with colleagues. Letting others know, even during a crunch period, that you are closing the laptop lid and stepping away from 6:30 to 8 p.m. to have dinner and spend time with your family before getting back online will help the lines from blurring while working at home.

It's worth remembering that work and home aren't in opposition—they're different aspects of life that constantly inform and influence each other. Succeeding as a dual-career couple in a way that enables both partners to be their best selves requires regularly examining your operating system. By keeping it intentional and updated, you will increase the probability of reaping the many opportunities your situation can bring.

Adapted from content posted on hbr.org, July 29, 2019 (product #H052KL).

Setting Goals as a Family

by Jackie Coleman and John Coleman

Quick Takes

- Establish an annual meeting to set goals
- Identify family, couple, and individual goals (even for kids)
- Use a set of questions to structure the conversation
- Hold each other accountable and share constructive feedback
- Check in on each other's progress

"Work" and "life" come up in our thoughts and conversation as separate and, all too often, in tension. We make annual resolutions, detailed daily plans, and to-do lists, but we do so as individuals, generally not sharing those plans or planning jointly with those closest to us. And we often think of our personal and professional goals as occupying distinct and separate spheres. But what if the work and home spheres could merge and actually improve the odds that we'll meet our goals?

Research shows that it's easier to achieve our goals when we're not trying to go it alone. One study found a positive correlation between participation in digital communities and reaching fitness goals.[1] Similarly, a study of rowers found that training together heightened their threshold for pain.[2]

For many of us, our closest and most trusted companion is a spouse. Couples in committed, long-term relationships often make plans to manage busy days or take fun trips, but rarely set resolutions or actively create long-term plans together. By not doing so, couples may actually be making it harder to achieve their goals. We decided to experiment with fully integrating our personal planning for the year. We've always informally mentioned our goals to each other, but this time around, we talked with intentionality about why we were chasing those goals, and how we planned to get there. By including each other in the process, we invited the other not only to be aware of what we plan to accomplish, but also to hold us accountable as we strive to reach these goals.

If you don't have a spouse or partner, you can still try these techniques with a family member, trusted colleague, close friend, or other ally. And parents might even think about including kids in some or all of these meetings to take advantage of their creativity and to help them focus and build life skills.

Our experience, combined with research we've evaluated and other couples we've consulted with, led to the following tips for effective planning within the context of a family.

Hold an Annual Board Meeting

Several years ago, we attended a seminar where speakers Rick and Jill Woolworth introduced the idea of an "annual meeting" for families—taking time at the end of each year to evaluate that year and plan for the next. Establishing this as a norm assures that goal setting happens on a set schedule rather than haphazardly or in isolation. For us, this happened over the holidays between Christmas and the new year, and included a discussion of the past year, how we performed against our goals, and how we felt about life as a couple, as individuals, and as a family as a whole. We wrote out our specific goals for the year and the habits we hoped to develop. Then we discussed them and how each of us could help the other achieve our goals. These annual meetings provide accountability, but more important, establish a vision for the year ahead. Then, as so many have advised, break these annual goals down into habits, monthly and weekly goals, and daily to-dos.[3]

By talking about your goals with your spouse or other allies and writing them down, you've already improved your odds of success. In *Yes!: 50 Scientifically Proven Ways to Be Persuasive*, authors Noah Goldstein, Steve Martin, and Robert Cialdini explain how making an active commitment directly affects action.[4] In one of the studies they reference, researchers found that out of a group of individuals who passively agreed to participate in a volunteer project, only 17% showed up to participate. Contrast that with those who agreed to volunteer through active means (writing it down, signing a contract, and so forth), 49% appeared as promised. Writing down specific goals and sharing them with your family is like signing a contract. It not only increases social accountability but also allows your spouse and others to think about specific ways in which they can support you in achieving your goals.

Set Joint Goals

The second essential component of annual planning is setting joint goals. What do you hope to achieve as a family? As a couple? As individuals (including your children)? What habits do you hope to develop together? Work-life balance is often cited as a key factor in job satisfaction, yet many of us struggle to achieve it. The people with whom you share your life are likely the best people to help you plan for balancing it. And joint goals can assure that your personal and professional pursuits are more fully aligned.

Hold Each Other Accountable

Once you've made your plans, help hold each other accountable. When you invite someone to join you in setting and striving for goals, you're not only asking them to cheer you on when you reach certain landmarks, you're also empowering them to point out when you're unfocused or offtrack. This requires recognizing that constructive feedback can be hard to hear and letting go of some ego and pride. To make the process easier and give your partner permission to hold you accountable, use a structured set of questions:

- What are 2–3 areas in which I'm falling short of my goals?

- What are 2–3 areas in which I'm succeeding?

- What's 1 thing I can do to improve this month?

Specifically working through questions like these helps focus the conversation and keep a balance between negative and positive feedback.

Check Your Progress

At the end of each month, check in on your progress using structured questions that work for your family. While making plans as a family is a good start, it's not enough to make things happen. Allow yourself regular checkpoints throughout the year to see where you are in developing habits and reaching your goals. Make it fun and something to look forward to. Order takeout or have a special meal. Keep the focus of the conversation on celebrating progress and identifying the setbacks of the month. Consider how you might build on things that are going well and brainstorm ways to get back on track when a goal or habit is off course. Some couples might be tempted to do this weekly, but monthly feedback seems to be the most realistic time frame. Once a month is enough time for you to have made meaningful progress but also frequent enough to allow you to course correct throughout the year.

• • •

Planning for both professional and personal goals with your spouse or other trusted ally can help you better care for one another, ensure that you're focused on the issues that matter most in the context of your family, enlist your biggest supporters in helping you achieve your goals and get things done, and teach your children about communication and partnership.

Adapted from "Increase the Odds of Achieving Your Goals by Setting Them with Your Spouse," on hbr.org, February 3, 2015 (product #H01UL0).

Navigating Trade-offs in a Dual-Career Family

by Monique Valcour

Quick Takes

- Focus your shared life—and dual careers—on what matters most
- Build and maintain consensus on what you want as individuals and as a family
- Agree on the kind of life you want—and stick to that shared vision even when circumstances change
- Experiment with ways of shouldering work, household duties, and childcare

When Patrick Pichette, Google's 52-year-old chief financial officer, retired to spend more time with his family, he gave voice to the sentiments of countless midcareer professionals in his retirement announcement when he asserted that "Life is wonderful" but it also involves a series of trade-offs between professional endeavors and commitments to family and community.

Making trade-offs is part of the daily juggle for dual-career families, as partners navigate their relationship, careers, family life, community commitments, and personal interests (since most don't have the option of chucking it all to travel the world together). Their lives are filled with negotiation. Whose career will take priority? If one partner accepts a job opportunity that requires the other partner to leave a good job and move elsewhere, for example, will the sacrifice be compensated in some way? How will domestic work (which may detract from career building) be divided up? And what if one or both partners become unhappy with the deal they've created? Can they renegotiate?

These challenges are made even more complex by the expectations society sets for working professionals and gender roles. We are all vulnerable to the cultural ideal of what a good employee looks like, or a high performer. Same goes for gender roles. There are cultural perceptions of what it means to be a good man or woman, husband or wife, father or mother. Combine the pressure from these norms with the reality of day-to-day life and it can be tough for even the healthiest couple to design and enact the lives *they* want to lead.

Research shows how these struggles play out. First of all, work is more likely to intrude into family life than the other way around.[1] It may seem impossible to say no to an awkwardly scheduled meeting or business trip, a high-profile project, or an urgent weekend email. On the other hand, cutting back on sleep, missing a family event, or working during vacation feels doable, even if it's stressful.

Consciously or unconsciously, couples adopt strategies for managing the demands of each career plus a shared domestic life.[2] There's the "one career/one job" pattern, in which the primary breadwinner's career is consistently prioritized, while the other partner's employment is made up of jobs that take lower priority. Most couples that start off with plans for an egalitarian partnership find that by midcareer the reality of their situation no longer matches their early-career intentions. A study of Harvard Business School graduates found that women ended up with lower career priority and a higher load of domestic responsibilities than they intended, while the opposite pattern held for men.[3]

How couples negotiate dual careers doesn't only affect success at work and the division of labor at home, but also how the partners feel about each other. Respondents in the study of Harvard Business School graduates who took a competitive approach to dual-career negotiations (for instance, by viewing one partner's gain as the other's loss) reported receiving less emotional support from their partner than those who took a cooperative approach (for instance, by being willing to compromise). Gender comes into play here as well: Women lost more emotional support than men when they negotiated competitively and gained less than men when they negotiated cooperatively. And both men and women who received less emotional support from their partner were more likely to feel frustrated, drained, and burned out in their relationship (though women were more resilient to lack of emotional support than men).

So, is it possible for couples to overcome these trends, to have two successful careers and to not sacrifice your relationship or your values in the process? The experience of ThirdPath Institute, a Philadelphia think tank that works with dual-career couples, shows that it is. Over the past 14 years, founder and president Jessica DeGroot has learned a great deal about how these couples can create and sustain two careers and a shared life that aligns with what matters most to the couple. She shared with me three lessons that stand out in particular.

Be intentional

The path of least resistance is simply to let work and traditional gender roles take over—whoever has the better (that is, higher-paying) job has first dibs on a career, for example, or the woman's career takes a back seat after they've had kids. Indeed, this is what happens when couples don't actively work to build and maintain consensus on what they want. ThirdPath creates communities of support for what it calls "Pioneering Leaders" in order to help people bravely and creatively craft successful careers *and* rich personal lives, even when it feels like they're paddling against a strong tide of professional and societal norms. These communities convene to share ideas and experiences on how to pursue a work life that allows time for family and community. For instance, these leaders are very intentional about when they take on big assignments at work, carefully thinking through the potential implications on family life and only taking on extra commitments in ways and at times that are healthy for family as well as work.

Develop a common vision, then keep each other on track

You and your partner need to see eye to eye on the kind of life you want to lead and stick to it when circumstances change. For example, when couples have children, their intention of sharing responsibilities is often undermined by the demands of parenting and traditional gender roles. A common pattern is that mothers resist relinquishing control and fathers feel inadequate about their parenting abilities. Nate Lewis, a senior director at Eli Lilly and Company, and his wife, Robin, a sales vice president at GlaxoSmithKline, had always wanted to share family responsibilities and agreed that they should both be active, involved parents. During Robin's first business trip after the birth of their first baby, however, she called home with extensive instructions for Nate. Mindful of their agreement, Nate recalls saying, "Hey honey, if this is going to work, I need to learn how to parent while you're traveling." Honest conversations like this help couples renew their commitment to their shared vision. Just like practicing any other skill, keeping each other on track becomes easier over time.

Be willing to experiment

Michelle Hickox, the chief financial officer of Independent Bank in Texas, and her husband, Rob, both worked as accountants for many years, a field that can require long hours at tax time. Unlike most accountants, however, they found a way to achieve their desired vision of shared parenting by looking for ways to spread out workload and parent availability over the course of each year.

Michelle negotiated a flex-year schedule that was intense at tax time but light during the summer. Rob, meanwhile, negotiated a position that kept his schedule calm during tax season.

It is entirely possible for couples to have two successful careers and a fulfilling life, though it is unlikely to happen on its own. You'll make compromises—everyone does—but the key is to have open, honest, and regular conversations about what you both value most and to not let professional and societal constraints determine the trade-offs you're willing to make.

Adapted from "Navigating Tradeoffs in a Dual-Career Marriage," posted on hbr.org, April 14, 2015 (product #H020BW).

Can You Actually Afford to Change Your Career?

by Russell Clayton

Quick Takes

- Assess your—and your partner's—risk tolerance
- Review your spending to identify potential cuts
- Build or add to an existing emergency fund
- Flesh out alternative plans
- Test out your estimated salary
- Set and manage your family's expectations

Finances are what keep many of us from taking a leap and making a career change, especially when we have a partner and a family. Sure, our current job has lost its spark, but it's stable. Dependable. Reliable. Steady. We worry and wonder: *What would a career change do to our bank accounts? To our way of life? To our family?* We assume that a major reinvention would involve a gap between paychecks when we'd leave our job and break into a new field. Sometimes we think (or we know) that the career we'd love would fill our days with more meaning but pay us less (significantly less, even).

Take Steve. A well-respected HR manager in the public sector, leading his own recruitment team and earning a decent salary. Or Amanda, an elementary school teacher in the inner city with 11 years under her belt. Or Brandon, a rising star at a large, well-known nonprofit organization. Those who know these three individuals would likely have characterized their careers as successful. But Steve, Amanda, and Brandon all left those jobs and made a midcareer transition.

What drove them to abandon established careers, steady incomes, and security? For Steve, it was a desire to find meaningful work. Although he was doing well and liked his team and his company, he felt that his workdays alternated between feeling every minute tick by and putting out fires. While the pay was good, he felt like his role didn't have a deeper purpose. His heart wasn't in it.

Amanda found the instructional part of her job as an inner-city teacher extremely fulfilling, but she was discouraged by paperwork and trying to "teach to the test." She noted, "I was only teaching 30% of the time, and the rest I was filling out forms." Gradually her frustration with these aspects of her job mounted, and she became burned out.

Brandon took the leap and left his stable nonprofit job to seek a better work-life balance. He wasn't intending to change his career until a conversation with his young daughter revealed that she felt as though he worked too much and spent too little time with her. While he was making significant improvements to his organization's way of doing business, the 80-hour weeks were wrecking his home life. He had to make a change.

Like Steve, Amanda, and Brandon, we're all drawn to career change for different reasons. But for many of us, worry about the potential financial risk in such a change turns into a roadblock we never surmount. While every situation is different, here are some factors to consider that may help reduce your financial concerns and make a radical move feel more achievable.

Try Living on Your New Income

If you're worried that your new job will pay less, test out your estimated salary. Take what you anticipate earning, and live on that for two to four months. Better yet, live on *less* than you anticipate earning. This will give you a realistic picture of what life would look like, from an income perspective, in your new career. For starters, review your budget to see where your current income is going. If you don't already have a budget, take a look at the past six months of your credit card bills and checkbook and debit card logs to see where you've been spending. Once you have a budget in place, go over your expenses—both fixed and discretionary—to see where you could trim. How much should you cut back? That depends on the anticipated size of your income reduction. If your new career would pay you 90% of what you make in your current gig, then you can probably manage the transition by reducing what you spend on groceries, canceling your cable TV service, or forgoing meals out. If your new career will result in a sizable pay cut, you'll need to be more aggressive. Look at your major spending categories to identify cost-saving opportunities. Are there more-affordable housing options in your area? Can you cut your commuting costs by using public transportation? While you may be reluctant to take such drastic steps for an experiment, use this period to explore alternatives and assess the impact of making changes. Say you want to downsize your home to reduce your monthly payment. How feasible is it to find cheaper housing in your area? If the real estate market where you live is down, it could be difficult to get out of your current home.

When Amanda planned to quit her teaching job, she knew the move to working part-time at a nonprofit would come with an approximate $30,000 reduction in her salary based on an exploratory meeting she'd had with the organization's leader. Amanda was pregnant but planned to go back to work part-time immediately following her daughter's birth. However, complications during her pregnancy forced her to take an extended period of strict bed rest. Her teaching benefits didn't cover short-term disability. She could not work; she did not earn an income. "This accidental trial run was rough, and we had to watch every penny . . . but it showed us that we *could* make it on less money," she reported. Though Amanda didn't choose the timing or duration of her trial run, you can map out an intentional reduced budget for a set period of time to get a realistic picture of what life might be like if you earn less.

At the end of your trial, revisit your budget or your banking statements to see how you did. What was the resulting impact on what you have saved—and what you owe? How did it feel? Are you willing to make those cutbacks more permanent? Take this opportunity to scrutinize your spending to see if there are additional expenses, like Netflix and Amazon Prime memberships, that could be eliminated.

Create an Emergency Fund

What if something unexpected happens in your new career? Or what if you can't sell your home? Building or adding to an existing emergency fund will help ease the stress and worry of beginning a new career. A good rule of thumb is to have three to six months' worth of living expenses saved up. While this advice is somewhat standard among financial advisers, aim for the higher end of that spectrum to give you some breathing room, just in case your transition doesn't go as planned. The more financial cushion you have, the more time you can take to find another job if it comes to that.

So how can you build an emergency fund? For starters, you could earmark your income tax return or yearly bonus. As you try out your new salary, take the dollars per month you've cut from your expenses as part of your experiment and add it to your emergency fund. Or extend your trial run and choose to live frugally for a longer period so you can stash away more cash. Steve and his wife chose that option to save money before he returned to graduate school. In addition to the usual cost-saving measures, they sold one of their cars and shared one car between them. This not only got rid of a monthly car payment, it also cut down on what they spent on gas, insurance, and maintenance. Your adventure into frugal living might look like Steve's, or you might cut costs elsewhere. If you're driving a vehicle with a high monthly payment, can you trade it in for something cheaper? Can you limit discretionary expenses (coffee, subscriptions, memberships)? Can you think outside the box and consider far-reaching ways you could save money? Maybe you could adopt a minimalist wardrobe, with a few essential, interchangeable, easy-care pieces. Doing so would allow you to reduce your clothing allowance and curb your dry-cleaning bills.

Of course, living frugally requires a lot of motivation. It sounds dreadful. It can feel dreadful. Focusing on *why* you're making these cuts can help. You're scrimping to have the career you desire instead of a job that simply pays the bills. Tap your support system for ideas to save—and to cope. And be sure to reward yourself once in a while. Celebrate your successes. For every $1,000 saved toward your emergency fund, treat yourself to something nice (but reasonable), like a dinner out.

Assess Your Household's Risk Tolerance

How do you feel about risk? How does your spouse feel about it? Everyone's tolerance for risk is different. Take Brandon. He considers himself risk averse, so when he made the move from nonprofit leadership to starting his own business, he did so with caution. He built up his emergency cushion by pulling his child out of daycare and keeping her at home with him. Once he'd launched his business, he continued to mitigate risk by being extremely selective about which clients he'd take on. To provide a level of job security and predictable income, Brandon only contracted with organizations that would agree to let him manage their conferences for two or more years. Likewise, Margaret, a single mother of two who is admittedly risk averse, did not transition from tenure-track college instructor to HR consultant until she found a job with the salary she needed. Had the money not been right she would not have made the move. She knew her budget and her risk tolerance; she did not have a partner's salary or health insurance to fall back on. She wasn't willing to compromise or to put her family in a bad spot just to make the change.

Assessing how comfortable you are with risk will help you see which choices are good for you—and which ones you should leave on the table. Quantify your level of risk tolerance by taking one of the many self-assessments you can find online, such as the financial risk tolerance questionnaire developed by Virginia Tech's Ruth Lytton and University of Georgia's John Grable. If your risk tolerance is fairly low but your proposed career change is one that will reduce your income by 75%, then you'll probably want to rethink your choice. On the other hand, if a questionnaire suggests you have a high tolerance for risk, a drastic reduction in salary may not be a deterrent for you.

Create a Backup Plan

Knowing how you feel about risk will also give you a sense of how solid your backup plan should be. If you're highly cautious about change, reduce your stress by fleshing out a plan B (and C and D, if necessary). Take all of the reflecting and imagining you did to get to where you are to consider what you might do if your new gig doesn't work out as you'd hoped. Steve, Amanda, and Brandon all had working spouses whose income provided a safety net during their career transitions. Beyond that, all three noted that their extended families had offered financial assistance if necessary. Beyond money, Steve, Amanda, and Brandon maintained their relationships with colleagues in their prior workplaces and industries. Knowing that they existed and could be tapped into in the event that they needed to return to their old field provided some reassurance.

In addition to maintaining ties with former colleagues in your network, stay abreast of what's happening in your old industry. If you're leaving the mortgage loan field, keep up with regulations and policies that govern that area. Or if you're leaving an industry that requires a certification (such as a CPA), maintain any licenses or credentials until you're well entrenched into your new career. You'll mitigate your stress and risk during the transition and give yourself a greater opportunity to return to your former industry should you need to.

Manage Expectations

Check in with your family members to discuss the implication of your change on their lives. These conversations should focus on schedule adjustments, income variances, and spending habits that will make the transition a success. Setting expectations for what your new life will look like—especially financially—will leave room for few surprises and less resulting disappointment once income levels change. Amanda, Brandon, and Steve all had multiple conversations with their spouses over time before they switched careers. Amanda and her husband were accustomed to dining out a few times per week while she was employed as a teacher. So they talked about discretionary spending they'd eliminate—meals out—in order to live on the reduced income her career transition would entail. When she changed jobs and dining out became a rare treat instead of a regular occurrence, it took getting used to, but no one was caught off guard.

Steve's career change required different stages of setting and managing expectations with his wife, as his transition came in two phases that took place over four years. First he moved from HR manager to college instructor, which came with a $15,000 per year reduction in income. After holding that job for a year and a half, he returned to graduate school full-time—going without a steady income for three years. Steve and his wife deliberated for a full year before he moved into the unpaid student phase of his career change. "While we did roll the dice financially, we arrived at that point mutually," Steve notes. "We knew what we were getting into." To assess their situation, Steve and his wife looked into apartment rental prices and cost-of-living data for the various cities where he applied to graduate school. They also looked at employment data in those cities to assess his wife's chances of finding a job if they were to move there. All this research and discussion paid off, as they discovered they were willing and able to live frugally in a handful of the cities where he applied to graduate school.

The financial implications of a career change weigh heavily on the mind of anyone considering doing something different. You'll have to do some deep thinking, conduct some tough conversations, and make some lifestyle changes. But moving to a career that makes you happy to get up and go to work every day will help you remember that your short-term sacrifices are in service of your long-term goals. Your transition won't happen overnight or come without bumps in the road, but don't lose hope. It can be done.

Adapted from content posted on hbr.org, August 29, 2018 (product #H04HNP).

Section 3

Away We Go!

Live Elsewhere for Your Job

How to Decide Whether to Relocate for a Job

by Rebecca Knight

Quick Takes

- Ask, Who do I want to become?
- Propose a temporary stint to test out the new location
- Consider the long-term impact on you and your family
- Find out what your next move would be
- Solicit advice from trusted peers

Sometimes the perfect job isn't down the street, but rather thousands of miles—or perhaps even an ocean—away. If you're offered a job in a different location, how do you know if it's worth relocating? Who should help you make the decision? And, how do you weigh the potential upsides like money and opportunity against costs like the impact on your family or the loss of your existing network?

What the Experts Say

Whether or not to relocate for a new role is a big decision both professionally and personally. "There are so many factors to consider," says Jennifer Petriglieri, an associate professor at INSEAD and author of *Couples That Work: How Dual-Career Couples Can Thrive in Love and Work*. "What's the opportunity? What's the longevity [of the job]? And what's the family situation?" Indeed, the decision is especially complicated if you have a partner and children, says Matthew Bidwell, an associate professor at Wharton whose research focuses on patterns of work and employment. "It's not just, what does this mean for *your* career, but what does this mean for *our* family?" he says. Relocating for a job can often be "great for your personal and professional development," but it's also "a risk and a leap into the unknown." Here are some ideas to help you think through whether the move is right for you.

Think holistically

When you're wrestling with a big decision, "there's a temptation to get out an Excel spreadsheet and weigh the pros and cons," says Petriglieri. But this is an instance where Excel comes up short. "When you're choosing one life over another, it becomes an identity choice: Who do I want to become? What kind of family will we be?" The job is only one piece of the puzzle. Consider your "holistic happiness and satisfaction." Think about the lifestyle that the new location affords or lacks. Are you suited for small-town life? Or do you prefer a big city? Do you want to spend your weekends traveling? Or do you want to feel rooted in a community? The answers to these questions will help you uncover what this "move means for you, your partner, and your children," she says. "When it's a difficult choice, it means that no option is clearly better than the other." Try to think beyond the immediate move, suggests Bidwell. "Ask, What is best for us in the long term?"

Talk through the move with your partner a lot . . .

The most important person in this equation is your partner, says Bidwell. "The big issue is what does this move do to your partner's career?" Will they be able to find meaningful work in the new place? If not, how big of a setback will it be? "There's quite a lot of research showing that people suffer from putting their career on hold," he says. If your partner won't have a job in the new location, "the move brings up other issues because you're taking them away from their support network." He points to a certain unhappiness known as trailing spouse syndrome. "You have a new job, new office, and all sorts of new people to meet; your spouse has been dropped in the middle of nowhere and knows no one." Petriglieri notes that trailing spouses often bear the brunt of move-related household tasks. "It's tough," she says. "Whenever you move, for the first six months, you are in the trenches." And it takes a huge toll. "Research on why relocations fail always points to the unhappiness of the trailing spouse," she says.[1]

. . . And talk to your kids a little

"It's possible to move at any time with kids, but certain ages are more difficult than others," says Petriglieri. Many people, for instance, are reluctant to move when their kids are teenagers; when kids are younger than eight, the prospect of uprooting them is much less daunting. Petriglieri says that while obviously you need to speak with your children about a potential move, she cautions, "there is a danger of consulting them too much because it brings up a lot of anxiety unnecessarily." Children, she says, "have a harder time imagining what their life will be like" in a new place. They might become resistant to move, which will make things much harder on you. Bidwell concurs: "The kids may complain, but they will adjust." Keep your eyes on the prize. The relocation "is a potentially enriching and stimulating experience."

Consider your development

Moving to a new job in a new city is a surefire way to help "round out" your skills and experience, says Bidwell. "You'll get to know people from different parts of the company; you'll be exposed to new ideas; you'll be able to build a broader network." And if you're relocating overseas, you'll gain an "understanding of a different culture." Indeed, in many organizations, "some form of international experience is necessary to get that top job." But recognize that the relocation poses "long- and short-term trade-offs" to your development. For instance, "the new cultural context you're learning comes at the expense of your loss of network back home." To keep that from happening, "make sure you're on the radar screen" with your home office "having conversations with all the right people on a regular basis," Bidwell says.

Find out what's next . . .

You must also think about the opportunity within the context of your long-term professional path. "Most companies are not likely to offer you a relocation unless there's something pretty big in it for you, meaning a significant promotion and raise," Petriglieri says. But the question you need to ask is, "What's the next move after this?" If, say, you're an American considering a three-year stint in London or Paris, that question is less complicated. "It's a no-brainer that you will probably return to the U.S." But if you're asked to "head up operations in Denver or Cleveland," the calculation is a little trickier. And yet, while it's important to think about next steps, you need to have reasonable expectations, says Bidwell. "There is a tension there," he says. "On one hand you want to have a conversation about where do I go after this? But realistically, the company can't give you a definitive answer." And besides, "career paths tend to be haphazard for most of us."

. . . And whether there's an escape hatch

Worst-case scenario: You and your family are miserable. What then? "You need to think about an escape hatch if you don't like it or if it doesn't gel for your family," says Petriglieri. It somewhat depends on the location itself. "When you are relocating to a hub city and it doesn't work out, there are often other options, but if you're moving somewhere more isolated, it's harder." The specifics of the role you're considering are also key. Make sure you're not professionally pigeonholing yourself "by taking on a specialist role," she says. Another danger, says Bidwell, is "staying too long" in your adopted city. "There's a risk that if you stay in a role for a long time, you become a specialist for that region," he says. This is why he recommends "talking with your partner beforehand about how long you're going for and agree on an exit plan."

Seek advice

It's often helpful to solicit input from others—with one caveat. "You want to talk with people who are not too close to the issue," says Petriglieri. Your boss, for instance, may try to convince you to go. After all, there's presumably "a business need" and a reason you've been asked to move in the first place. And friends and family members have a vested interest in your choice. "No one is neutral, and these conversations can become charged." Ideally, she says, you should talk with "a group of trusted peers" who "have similar family issues and similar career aspirations." These people can be "a good sounding board" as you evaluate your options. Bidwell agrees. He suggests seeking advice from colleagues who've done similar stints as well as others in your industry. "You need moderately unbiased views of what to expect."

Request a tryout

If you're uncertain, it may be worth asking your organization if you could do a temporary stint or job swap in the proposed location before making a big move, says Petriglieri. "Relocations are extremely costly," she says. "Failed relocations are even worse." She says companies are "increasingly willing to allow employees to do short-term relocations or secondments" to maximize the likelihood of success. In essence, your employer would be giving you a chance "to try before you buy." Even if your organization does not offer this opportunity, "you can always ask," says Bidwell.

Don't overanalyze

Whether or not to relocate is a big decision—but beware of analysis paralysis, overthinking a situation so that a decision is never made or one is made by default. Try to have perspective. "As you get older, there are very few decisions in life where you don't feel some ambivalence," says Petriglieri. "A career is long," she adds. "We can all afford a few adventures, and we have plenty of time to experiment and explore." However, don't assume that this is your one chance at trying something new. If you're miserable, you can course correct, says Bidwell. "You have to take risks in your career," he says. "Sometimes it doesn't work out, and so, you figure out what to do next."

Case Study: Consider the Next Phase of Your Career

Anne Chow spent the first 15 years of her career at AT&T, earning promotion after promotion, at the company's headquarters in New Jersey. "It was very easy to move around the company without geographically moving my family," she says.

In 2005, after AT&T was purchased by SBC, Anne was asked to move to Texas, where the new company was based. At the time, Anne had young children, and she was reluctant to move away from her parents. She was also hesitant about Texas itself. "I am a Jersey Girl and East Coast through and through," she says.

She declined to move. But by 2014, her perspective had changed. Her career was going well; her kids were older—middle school and high school; and her husband was retired. "I was questioning what I wanted to do next and what I wanted the next phase of my career to look like," she says.

She briefly considered outside opportunities, but after 24 years at AT&T, she wanted to "double-down on [her] commitment to the company." She broached the topic of moving with her family. "My husband was supportive, and my children were in," she recalls. "I declared myself mobile to move to Texas."

Shortly thereafter, the CEO tapped her to take on a new job leading sales operations and solutions. Once the relocation became real, her children changed their minds. "When we told the kids, they said we should go without them," she says.

She and her family had many long talks. "We talked about who we wanted to be," she says. "My husband had 51% of the vote. I was worried about his social infrastructure because it was his life that would change the most. The kids would assimilate."

After three years in Dallas, Anne has already had three different positions. Today she is the president of the national business.

Despite her career success, she admits that the first year was difficult for her spouse and kids. "It definitely made us a stronger family," she says. "But I don't know if we'll ever call it home."

Adapted from content posted on hbr.org, December 3, 2018 (product #H04OBG).

Making Your Expat Assignment Easier on Your Family

by Katia Vlachos

Quick Takes

- Recognize that relocating to a new country is a multistage process

- Frame the opportunity as a real choice

- Consider the implications on your careers, kids, extended family, and support networks

- Be open to trade-offs on timing, housing, and schooling

- Put your family first after the move

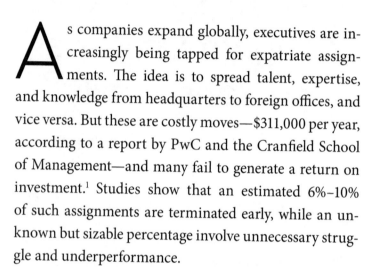

As companies expand globally, executives are increasingly being tapped for expatriate assignments. The idea is to spread talent, expertise, and knowledge from headquarters to foreign offices, and vice versa. But these are costly moves—$311,000 per year, according to a report by PwC and the Cranfield School of Management—and many fail to generate a return on investment.[1] Studies show that an estimated 6%–10% of such assignments are terminated early, while an unknown but sizable percentage involve unnecessary struggle and underperformance.

Where do expats go wrong? About 80% move with a partner or family, and it's often the partner or family's inability to acclimate to the new environment that causes the assignment to fail. According to surveys from BGRS, executives' most cited reason for giving up a foreign posting is "family concerns," including adjustment difficulties, partner career issues, children's education challenges, quality of life, and lack of practical support.[2]

However, in my seven years of working with expat assignees, I've found that, in most cases, such problems can be avoided. The key is to recognize that an international move is a multistage process—decision-making, preparation, moving, and, finally, settling in—each of which requires a systematic approach.

Deciding to Move

It is essential to gauge your partner's or family's interest in and commitment to the move, and to consider all its potential consequences together, as early as possible. First, frame the decision as a real choice—go or stay? And consider the degree of change: A relocation from Amsterdam to Brussels is very different from a relocation from Amsterdam to Guangzhou, China.

Next, focus on the pros and cons of each alternative, laying out the full implications for your career and your partner's, any children or extended family, and your social and support networks. Try to anticipate and discuss the impact of changes on family dynamics such as shifting from a dual-career marriage to one where a spouse stays at home, or replacing a grandmother babysitter with a professional nanny. These discussions will not only shape your decision about whether to accept the assignment but will also help shape expectations and avoid resentment later on.

Preparing for the Move

Identify the most important choices you need to make—timing, housing, support network, schooling—and think about how to make the new location "home" for each family member. Acknowledge the challenges of the transition and be explicit about the trade-offs involved in your choices (for example, putting kids in local schools may benefit their language skills but make the initial adjustment tougher). When it comes to picking a home, open and then narrow your options: House or apartment? Rent or buy? How big? City or country? Once your partner and/or children are all on the same page, start looking from afar.

You can also begin to build your new support system before you go. This includes institutions (childcare, health care), routines (schedules, activities), and people (friends, colleagues, caregivers, teachers, doctors, other service providers). Beyond the basics, you might want language lessons or career coaching. Study up on your destination, too: culture, history, people, what everyday life looks like. Reach out to expat organizations and forums for referrals and advice on dealing with practical needs, such as finding a pediatrician who does home visits or understanding recycling rules.

Finally, know and discuss how available you'll be during the transition. If work will consume you for your first few months in a new role, everyone needs to plan for that.

Making the Move

Leave well, so you can enter well. Budget time to say goodbye to loved ones and set up ways to keep in touch from abroad. Send out your new contact details, equip grandparents with tablets, set up social media groups, or start a family video diary and share it through a social channel that's popular with your friends and extended family. Stay connected with your partner and children. Make time for each other, and keep communicating, whether it's to express excitement or concern, hopes or fears. Ensure that everyone stays healthy by eating well, sleeping enough, exercising, and occasionally taking a break to relax. You can't spend every waking hour packing, unpacking, or handling logistics. Go for a walk; visit friends; have some fun. When anyone feels overwhelmed, think about how much you've already accomplished in executing the move.

Settling In

Even if you're extremely busy with work, know that family should come first in the critical first few months. Be alert and sensitive to their needs. Check in with them. Make sure they are supported. Listen, empathize, communicate. Be particularly sensitive to the possibility that your transition experience may differ from theirs.

As the assignee, you'll be familiar with your company culture and may already know some colleagues. Your partner and children are likely to feel much greater culture shock or isolation and will probably carry a heavier logistical burden. If your partner made career sacrifices to move with you, acknowledge this and seek out resources that will help them find new purpose and fulfillment.

If you have children, prioritize them. Help them unpack their boxes and create their own space in the new home, escort them to their new school, and sign them up for favorite activities so new routines are immediately established. Maintain or create rituals, such as a pizza-and-movie night on Fridays or bowling on weekends, that provide stability and comfort.

Finally, expand your social network. Go out, explore, and talk to your neighbors, or join a sports club, an expat organization, or the PTA, all while continuing to stay connected with family and friends back home through regular calls and invitations to come visit. Both sets of relationships, new and old, will improve the transition for everyone.

While nothing makes an expat move easy, approaching these four steps systematically can greatly improve your chances of making it a success.

Adapted from content posted on hbr.org, March 10, 2017 (product #H03IME).

10

Living Apart for Work

An interview with Danielle Lindemann
by Ania Wieckowski

Quick Takes

- Consider how flexible your job is

- Factors such as life stage, personality, and length of relationship will influence the success of your arrangement

- Stay connected with frequent contact through a variety of channels

- Have an end goal for your time apart

When spouses are offered career opportunities in different locations, they may choose to live apart. Some evidence suggests that this is happening more than ever before. HBR executive editor Ania Wieckowski talked with Danielle Lindemann, a sociologist at Lehigh University and the author of *Commuter Spouses*, to find out how these couples manage. Edited excerpts follow.

ANIA WIECKOWSKI: *What types of people are most likely to try a commuter marriage?*

DANIELLE LINDEMANN: Many of them are highly educated. It's counterintuitive, but when you're in a high-level job, employment possibilities become more limited, because only a few roles will make sense for you. One recent study, for instance, has shown that couples with graduate degrees are more likely to live apart than are couples with just college degrees.

AW: *What factors determine whether a couple can make this work?*

DL: According to the people I interviewed, the most crucial factor is life stage—especially whether you have kids. People who don't have children at home experience fewer complications. Personality also plays a role: You need a certain self-sufficiency and independence to make this work. Take into account how flexible your job is. If your company allows you to telecommute, or your career has built-in rhythms (such as slower summers in academia), it will be easier to live apart. Consider how far apart you'll be. One couple I studied was living a two-hour drive apart and seeing each other every weekend; they experienced fewer complications than the guy who was in a time zone 12 hours different from the one his wife was in—they had trouble figuring out when to even call each other. Finally, take the temperature of your relationship. If it's new, or if you're struggling a bit, living apart can exacerbate the problems.

AW: *Does technology make this easier?*

DL: Yes. Many professionals can stay in semiconstant contact with their spouses, texting throughout the day. Frequency of contact is important: One study of workers on oil rigs who were out of touch with their families for days at a time found it was really tough on their relationships. For most couples, phone and texting are the most important channels of communication—even more than video chat. Couples who communicate effectively think about which channel to use depending on the kind of information they're sharing. If they're making plans and need to get details across, they send an email, but if it's a more emotional conversation, they'll get on the phone. Many modern communication tools are what my colleague Raelene Wilding has called sunny-day technologies, because they work well when your relationship is going well but can do more harm than good for unsteady relationships.

AW: *Should couples go into these arrangements with an endgame?*

DL: Most do anticipate living with their spouses again. Some have a specific date in mind, often tied to a career milestone such as the end of a medical residency or retirement. They view having an end goal as a positive thing. Those with a hazier end date tend to experience more anxiety.

AW: *What happens when these couples move back in together?*

DL: There's an adjustment period. They're used to having their own space, and suddenly there are turf wars; they're used to doing things in a certain way, and suddenly that creates friction. This is similar to what's been found in research about military spouses coming home from deployments.

AW: *Are there any benefits to living apart from your spouse—other than being able to take the job you want?*

DL: Yes! Some people find that they're recharged with the excitement they felt when dating. Others appreciate the absence of all the little tensions that arise from sharing a space. This is particularly important for women, who cherish their newfound independence—having their own space and their own time. Some couples say that their communication improves when they're apart because their distance becomes a forcing function. If you have a call scheduled with each other every night at 8:00, you have to talk about your day. Finally, the amount of work they can get done is one of the biggest benefits—they can work evenings when they want to without fear of impinging on family time. This is again particularly pronounced among women, unless they have children. One woman I interviewed said she didn't think she would have gotten tenure if she had been living with her husband.

Adapted from content published in Harvard Business Review, *September–October 2019 (product #S19054).*

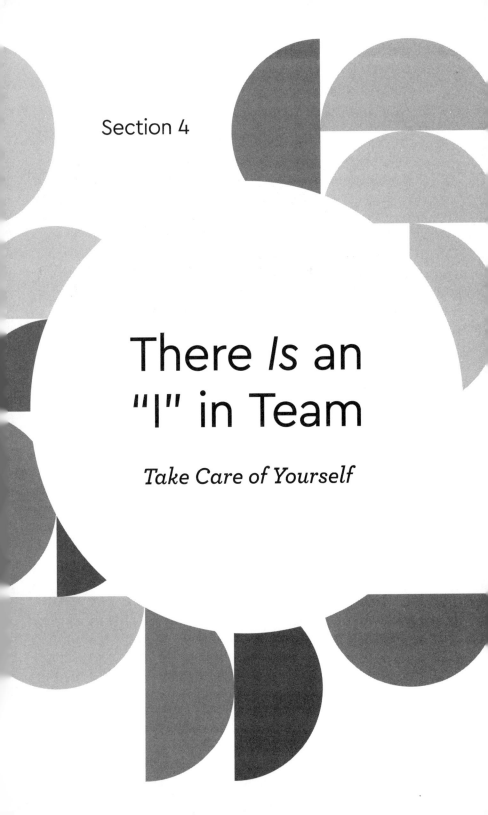

Section 4

There *Is* an "I" in Team

Take Care of Yourself

Make Time for "Me Time"

by Elizabeth Grace Saunders

Quick Takes

- Define what you need by thinking about your priorities
- Look for small pockets of time to take a microbreak
- Mark off time in your calendar to read, work out, or meditate
- Reinforce positive behaviors by planning in advance
- Advocate for yourself and your needs

D o you feel so busy that you don't have the bandwidth to think about your own needs, let alone do anything about them? Maybe you're constantly thinking about work, or worry that you're not proving yourself or your value if you aren't available 24/7 (especially if you're working remotely). Perhaps you're juggling childcare, eldercare, pet care, or other family commitments. Or maybe you're just caught up in the regular "life" tasks of paying bills, keeping a clean house, and managing the day-to-day. How do you carve out time for yourself, your health, and your needs when you're always on?

The first step is to stop, take a deep breath, and realize that the world doesn't rest completely on your shoulders. Many times the people around you could help more if you simply asked and spread out the responsibilities both professionally and personally. And in some cases, you need to let go and trust that everything will be OK, even if some tasks on your list are done imperfectly or not at all.

The next step is to give yourself permission to take care of yourself now. If you put off self-care until work is less busy, your kids are back in school, your house is in order, or some other circumstances are exactly right, you may never get to it. But if you take a brief pause and go through these steps, you can begin to take care of yourself, even when it feels like the responsibilities at home and at work never end.

Define What You Need

When it comes to health and happiness, different people have different needs. But there are some universal truths. We all need the basics of sleep, physical movement, and sufficient food. And to thrive, most require quality time with people, time in nature, time for spiritual connection, and time doing something that brings joy.

Take a moment to define what you need and what you want. Ask yourself:

- How many hours of sleep are sufficient for you to be alert throughout the day?

- What kind of physical movement keeps you feeling in shape and pain-free?

- What nourishment keeps up your energy and makes you feel satisfied?

- Which people do you enjoy spending time with?

- How can you find ways to be outside?

- How can you connect with yourself and find your spiritual center?

- What activities give you joy (a hobby, reading, volunteering, etc.)?

You don't need to apologize for your needs. They're valid. And it's also OK to have wants, even when your life is very full.

Determine What You Can Do

At certain stages of your life—when work is particularly busy, you're supporting a kid through a school challenge, or you're going through a big change like a move—you may not be able to do all the self-care you would prefer. But you can still do something.

Think through what's reasonable given your current situation. For example, maybe you can't guarantee that you'll sleep through the night given the ages of your kids, but you can go to bed an hour early to give yourself some margin. Maybe it's not possible to train for a half marathon right now, but you could take half an hour to run a few times a week. Perhaps you can't see your friends as much as you'd like in person, but you can give them a phone call while you're cooking dinner or running errands. Take a look at your schedule and where there may be small pockets of time. What would work to fulfill your needs now, within the time you have?

Set the Time

If you feel as though there is always more you could be doing, you'll need to consciously set aside time for self-care. In doing so, you will clearly give yourself permission that this is an important and appropriate thing to do now. Scheduling helps you to see where self-care fits into your day, and how other essential activities have their places around it.

For example, I have a get-ready-for-bed alarm that goes off on my phone from Sunday through Thursday night to remind me that sleep needs to be the priority. I have a time set aside in the morning to work out—in my case, swimming. And I have times planned for prayer, family, and friends. You could also put in time for reading during lunch or alongside your child before bed. Take a short nap or do a brief meditation during the afternoon energy slump, or go on a walk as a household after dinner before settling down in front of the TV. Or plan nights to get takeout so that you save the cooking time and can fit in an errand or exercise video.

Think through when you want to make taking care of yourself a priority. Not only does self-care reenergize you, but it can also motivate you to stop wasting time on unsatisfying activities. It's less tempting to scroll through Instagram in the afternoon if you could use those few minutes for a quick mindfulness exercise or you know you need to get your work done by 5 p.m. to get in your workout before dinner.

Prep Yourself

To make this happen, you'll need to have resolved that your self-care time is sacred and that you're going to follow through on it. That means eliminating hurdles and putting in items that reinforce positive behaviors. For example, if you want to exercise more, clean off the treadmill, have your favorite workout videos queued up, or sign up for exercise classes in advance where there's a penalty if you cancel last-minute. Or if you want to eat healthier, have a standard weekly grocery list of nutritious food, remove unhealthy food from your kitchen, and have some quick premade or takeout options for those days when you're in a pinch. You could also join a challenge where you have accountability and support, and sometimes even win prizes for achieving your self-care goals.

To reinforce positive behaviors in the moment, think about the details in advance. Eliminate the friction between yourself and your goal. Lay out your workout clothes by the foot of your bed—or even wear them to bed as pajamas—to save time before going out for a run. Or install an app on your phone and computer that locks you out at a certain time as a reminder to get sufficient sleep. Remember what you're doing and why it's important to you, so when you're tired or feeling unmotivated, you have the gumption to follow through.

Be Clear with Others

Finally, prep others. If your spouse tends to stay up late watching TV, let them know when you need to watch the final show and then head to bed. If your kids get up super early and are old enough to safely play by themselves for a little while, explain that you'll be exercising, reading, or sipping a cup of coffee on the porch in the morning, and they can join you if they like or play until you're done.

Set similar boundaries at work. If someone suggests an early-morning or late-night meeting and it's negotiable, ask for a time that will work better for your sleep schedule or other self-care routines. And if you find yourself perpetually fielding last-minute requests from your boss or clients, have a conversation with them about the possibilities. Could you be informed of upcoming needs sooner? Could you receive work earlier? Could deadlines be negotiated? To have time for self-care, you'll need to advocate for yourself and your needs to make it happen.

I can't guarantee that you will ever feel really "off." But you can take steps to make sure that you put focus and attention on taking care of yourself each day. "Always on" doesn't have to mean you must sacrifice your needs. It just means sometimes finding the time to make sure that your focus is on yourself.

Adapted from content posted on hbr.org, April 1, 2021 (product #H069LV).

12

How to Communicate Your Self-Care Needs to Your Partner

by Jackie Coleman

Quick Takes

- Find a time to talk that is free of distractions and relatively calm

- Use "I feel" statements to avoid blame or criticism

- Listen actively—and be willing to compromise

- Do regular checkups on your relationship and family

The morning rush: shower, eat breakfast, get the kids dressed, start the day. The workday: meetings, then calls, then more meetings. The evening: dinner, baths, bedtimes. Climb into bed, only to start over again. Lather, rinse, repeat.

As a working parent with a seemingly endless array of responsibilities, it can be hard to make space for yourself. The tendency to focus all your energy on work or family and put your own needs on hold is the norm. And extreme or unusual circumstances—like the recent Covid pandemic—can only make this more difficult. As parents and children found themselves stuck at home juggling work, school, and entertainment, it felt as if there was even less time to dedicate to their own needs.

But the benefits of taking care of yourself, whether that's physically, emotionally, spiritually, or mentally, are undeniable. It's the whole "adjust your oxygen mask first before assisting another" principle. My husband, John, and I call it creating a "third space"—space outside of home and work to explore interests, decompress, and find personal fulfillment. This can lead to decreased anxiety, increased productivity, and overall higher levels of life satisfaction.

But even when you know the benefits of focusing on your own physical and mental health, it can be challenging to communicate your personal needs to your partner. Feelings of guilt or shame may prevent these conversations, but not sharing your feelings and needs can lead to resentment, exhaustion, and contempt. And failing to reserve time for yourself can make you less happy and less effective both at work and at home.

So how can you better communicate to your partner a need for a third space or personal time? As a wife, mother of three, and former marriage counselor who has worked with numerous couples, I see a few distinct ways.

First, know what you need. Take two minutes right now to list what third space would most benefit you. Jot down whatever comes to mind. The stereotypical picture of self-care is a vision of someone lounging in a white bathrobe with cucumbers over their eyes. And while some spa time can be great relaxation for some people, there are so many other possibilities. Is it taking 15 minutes after work to sit and decompress before jumping in to help with the kids? Maybe it's enjoying a couple of hours on a weeknight or weekend to read a book for fun. Research has found that simply anticipating an activity or event has many benefits.[1] So maybe you don't need weekly time but would enjoy having something big to look forward to, like a future weekend away with friends or a night alone in a hotel. I have personally taken up guitar and voice lessons, which at first seemed self-indulgent (read:

Create a Third Space

by Jackie Coleman and John Coleman

When professionals have families, their entire lives can revolve around their responsibilities at work and at home. Busy executives run home to help with kids (changing diapers or shuttling preteens to soccer games) or to do the little things that keep a home humming, like laundry, yard work, or cooking. But having a third space outside of work and home can help enormously with stress management.

Each partner in a relationship should maintain habits and times that allow them to explore their interests, relax and seek fulfillment, and find space outside of home and work. These spaces are different for everyone—quiet cafés, virtual book clubs, trout streams, karate classes, poker nights—but they are important for maintaining our identities and our sense of peace.

Make the sacrifice of offering your partner a third space to find themselves, maintain their friendships, and explore their interests, and ask that they do the same for you. This may mean taking over as solo parent on a regular basis—prepping meals, assisting with schoolwork, even covering bath- and bedtime. Third spaces mean no person runs from responsibility to responsibility without having time to breathe.

Adapted from "Don't Take Work Stress Home with You," on hbr.org, July 28, 2016 (product #H0315M).

guilt!) but has quickly become life-giving. Even virtual lessons can offer you the space you need. Look at your list and highlight what sticks out to you the most. Then consider whether the top few choices are feasible for your available time and finances, and whether they'll truly recharge you.

Now that you have thought through your own needs and desires, how do you actually have a successful and productive conversation? Consider these tactical suggestions.

Timing is everything

There are moments during the day when a conversation of substance would fail miserably: the minute your spouse or partner signs off from work or walks in the door, the bath-time rush, and the "witching hour(s)" getting kids fed and ready for bed, to name a few. To avoid this, set aside a time together that is free of distractions, relatively calm, and likely to be when neither of you is overtired. The best approach is to make it fun and think of it not as a way to challenge your partner, but as a way to connect. John and I love grabbing a snack and sitting together by our little pond in the front yard after we finish the kids' bedtimes. These moments are peaceful and never feel onerous. Finding this type of breather provides the right context for a promising conversation.

Remember you're playing for the same team

Approach the conversation in this way: You are your spouse's advocate and supporter, just as they are yours. And you both have one another's health and well-being in mind. John Gottman, a prominent researcher on marital success, encourages a "soft startup." This means handling the conversation with gentleness and avoiding blame or criticism. You can do this by using "I feel" statements that focus on your own thoughts and needs instead of universal and accusatory statements like "You always" or ". . . never," etc. Realize it is much easier to hear, "I am feeling really tired and burned out lately, and I was thinking about how much I would love to learn to paint. What do you think?" versus "You always get to do what you want and never let me have a moment to myself." These are extreme examples, but one encourages partnership, while the other sparks defensiveness.

Actively listen

Really try to hear the heart behind your partner's statements and don't just listen to respond. It can take effort to set aside your personal agenda, but after taking time to think about what your spouse's needs or wants might be, this will be easier to do. When your partner says something, be curious, paraphrasing what you hear (even if you don't agree). And ask for clarification by saying something like, "That's interesting. Tell me more." Aim to truly understand how your partner feels. Creating an empathetic atmosphere will encourage understanding in the relationship.

It's about give-and-take

You want something, but be willing to give a little, too. Relationships aren't about demands. They're about mutual understanding, compassion, and sacrifice. While you have thoughts on what you need, be open to what your spouse verbalizes, too. And I'd encourage you to take it one step further. Preemptively take some time to think through what your partner might be needing or wanting, and incorporate these thoughts into the conversation. Demonstrate that you have been considering them. Empathy goes a long way in deepening connection.

Do regular relationship checkups

It is so much easier to talk about things in a casual way when resentment, frustration, or utter exhaustion hasn't developed. Doing regular check-ins (like our nightly post-bedtime hangouts by the pond) provides a natural time and space to ask how the other is doing and to share ways that could help us flourish more. We have gotten in the habit of doing a weekly date day on a Saturday or

Sunday to go on a hike together or explore a new part of our city. You can take a walk around the neighborhood, have a special meal together after the kids are in bed, or even conduct a regular "board meeting" for your relationship and family. These conversations certainly don't need to take place every week, but having regular times mapped out is a helpful way to foster connection and open communication.

The day-in, day-out of raising children and fostering a thriving career can feel like that "lather, rinse, and repeat" cycle. But with some self-reflection, empathy for your partner, and thoughtful conversations, it can turn into "lather, *sing a bit in the shower*, rinse, repeat."

Adapted from content posted on hbr.org, April 22, 2020 (product #H05J42).

How Working Parents Can Prioritize Sleep

by Amie M. Gordon and Christopher M. Barnes

Quick Takes

- Set a consistent sleep routine—and stick to it
- Avoid talking about serious matters before bed
- Make the most of your family's sleeping schedules
- Shape your work schedule around your family
- Don't stress about a bad night's sleep

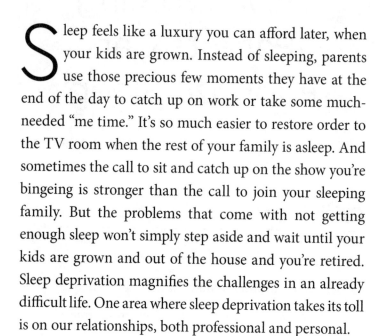

Sleep feels like a luxury you can afford later, when your kids are grown. Instead of sleeping, parents use those precious few moments they have at the end of the day to catch up on work or take some much-needed "me time." It's so much easier to restore order to the TV room when the rest of your family is asleep. And sometimes the call to sit and catch up on the show you're bingeing is stronger than the call to join your sleeping family. But the problems that come with not getting enough sleep won't simply step aside and wait until your kids are grown and out of the house and you're retired. Sleep deprivation magnifies the challenges in an already difficult life. One area where sleep deprivation takes its toll is on our relationships, both professional and personal.

The Impact of Poor Sleep

Research from across the globe has linked general sleep tendencies with relationship quality, showing that people who sleep worse experience less satisfying relationships, particularly with romantic partners.[1] People are more likely to fight with their partners after a poor night of sleep, and couples have more difficulty resolving conflicts if *either* partner slept worse the prior night.[2] The effects go the other way as well—people tend to sleep worse after fighting with their romantic partners.[3] This creates the possibility of a vicious cycle in which poor sleep begets conflict, and conflict begets poor sleep. Additionally, research suggests children who are exposed to more marital conflict tend to sleep worse, which may have further negative effects on the parents' sleep.[4] In contrast, children whose parents have higher-quality relationships tend to sleep better.[5]

Sleep also plays a role in how we relate to our children. One study found that mothers who had more-disrupted sleep were less sensitive to their 18-week-old infants than those who had more continuous sleep.[6] Good sleep may also be a protective factor; both parents and children who sleep better are more resilient in the face of stressors.[7] Overall, getting the sleep we need helps us have better relationships with our children.

Poor sleep has consequences in the workplace, too. Leaders who report sleeping worse tend to engage in more abusive behaviors toward their employees (such as yelling at them in front of their colleagues) and have damaged relationships with those employees. Sleep-deprived leaders are also less charismatic and generally less effective in their leadership roles. Research indicates that overall, businesses benefit when employees are well rested.[8]

Everybody's Tired

The people in your life are likely just as tired as you are, so if your partner forgets to call you on their way home from work, assume it's because they had a difficult workday and not because they don't value your time. If your child is giving only one-word answers at dinner, remind yourself they may just be exhausted from an active day at school and not uninterested in what you have to say. And when your colleague forgets to confirm a meeting, check to see how they're doing personally before writing them off as unreliable.

Don't jump to conclusions or react unhappily. Give your family and colleagues the benefit of the doubt. Perhaps they could just use a good night's sleep.

Deprioritizing sleep is one way to deal with the heavy demands on a working parent's limited time, but the consequences are clear: Both at home and in the workplace, relationships are worse when people don't sleep.

Establish Habits for Better Sleep

So, what is a time-famished working parent to do? It's not easy, but working parents can get a better night's sleep. Here are a few evidence-based tips to help you take care of yourself and create good sleeping practices—even when it seems like there is no time to do so. Getting good sleep won't give you more time in your day, but it will help you make better use of the time you have. You know the basics like limiting your exposure to blue light at night and keeping screens out of your bedroom. But here are some additional practices to consider.

Make sleep a priority

Recognize that your days will feel more productive if you get enough sleep, which can give you a sense of having more time. There's always the desire to do one last thing and put off going to bed, but a good night's sleep will give you the resources you need to deal with the demands of daily life. Figure out how much sleep you need to feel well rested (the recommendation in the United States is seven to nine hours for adults, though occasionally people require more or less).[9] Decide what time you need to wake up in the morning, then count backward. Set a bedtime alarm, giving yourself an extra 30 minutes to an hour to unwind and get ready for bed each night. Creating a relaxing bedtime routine for the whole family (dim lights, relaxing music, stories in bed) might be one way to get everyone to wind down together.

Set a consistent sleep routine for yourself and your children

One of the best ways to sleep well is to have a consistent sleep routine. This tells your body when to wake up and when to go to sleep so that it releases melatonin at the right time, making it easier to fall asleep and stay asleep. A consistent routine won't just get you more sleep; it will get you more high-quality sleep. Keep this routine on both the days you're working and the days you're not. Although it is enticing, using the weekends to do a major "catch-up" on sleep is actually counterproductive. Sleeping in late will feel good that day, but it throws off your body clock and fails to address the larger issue of having a consistent schedule that allows enough time for sleep on a daily basis. Children, even teens, get more sleep when parents help structure the child's sleep schedule.

Quit while you're ahead

We've all wanted to stay up just a little longer to finish the task we're working on or enjoy some quiet time alone. But if you're trying to work when it's time to go to bed, you're going to be less efficient and make more mistakes. Instead, stick to your bedtime so the next day you'll be refreshed, thinking clearly, and more productive.

Don't stress about those inevitable nights of poor sleep

While a consistent sleep routine is great, everyone experiences poor sleep at some point. Worrying about your sleep can become a problem of its own. Instead, recognize that your body is resilient and can handle short-term sleep problems, and find ways to de-stress before bed to help you relax and sleep well.

Work with Those Around You

Beyond ways to make your sleep more consistent and habitual, consider these relationship-based strategies to prevent the inevitable conflicts that can arise out of lack of sleep.

Don't talk about serious matters right before bed

Although you've likely been told to never go to bed angry, a good night of sleep might also help you deal more constructively with conflict. If you can, save serious matters for a time when you're both awake and have the energy to talk. This may seem impossible, but like sleep, building in time to talk when you aren't tired can help the rest of your relationship run more smoothly.

Make the most of different sleeping schedules

Having a different bedtime from your partner might seem problematic when your schedules don't overlap—whether those differences are due to personal preferences or work schedules. However, you may be able to leverage this difference by putting the person who wakes up early in charge of the morning routine and the night owl in charge of bedtime.

Explore flextime

If your job allows it, working from home or shaping your work schedule around your family might help you feel less stressed and sleep better.[10] For example, if you're an early riser, you might benefit from working at home in the morning before your family gets up and adjusting your hours accordingly. Consider being flexible with your family time as well. For instance, some families with full schedules might find that breakfast together works better than the traditional family dinner, so you can devote those evening hours to attending your children's extracurricular activities, cementing a toddler's bedtime routine, or unwinding after a long day, without the added stress of getting everyone—and a meal—to the table.

• • •

When you feel like you have no time to sleep is exactly when you need sleep the most. Finding a way to prioritize consistent, high-quality sleep can help you better navigate the demands of your everyday life, from better interactions with your family to better sleep for your children to better relationships at work.

Excerpted from content posted on hbr.org, March 31, 2020 (product #H05HR7).

Section 5

In Sickness and in Health

Take Care of Each Other

14

How to Not Fight with Your Spouse When You Get Home from Work

by Ed Batista

Quick Takes

- Realize that you and your partner may have different needs at the end of the day

- Expect that everyone will need some time to unwind

- Think about what "coming home" means for your spouse

- Consider the time it takes you and your partner to recover from challenges

- Talk about what you'd like to see happen when you first get home

My coaching clients have hard jobs with big responsibilities that generate lots of stress, and many of their spouses and partners have similarly demanding careers. And yet one of the most challenging experiences in their day doesn't occur at work, but in the first 15 minutes after they arrive home and greet each other.

When that initial personal encounter at the end of the workday goes well, it can help both parties feel a sense of care and appreciation that helps them unwind and feel better prepared for the following day. And yet it so often goes *badly*, creating frustration and a sense of disappointment that can poison the rest of the evening. There are several factors that make this such a difficult situation for couples to navigate.

Why We Can Clash

Different needs

Both parties are likely to be in different mental and emotional states with differing sets of personal needs, and while this may seem self-evident, it's striking how many couples forget this when they walk in the door. A common version of this is someone arriving home after a difficult day who needs some quiet and solitude before being ready to engage, only to meet a spouse or partner who arrived home earlier (or who spent the day there) and is eager to connect.

Even if both people arrive home simultaneously, they may have had vastly different experiences during the day—one person ran into a string of conflicts and had a terrible commute, while the other went from one triumph to another and enjoyed a peaceful journey home.

And even if both people had similar days, they may simply need very different things in response to those experiences. Some people need to talk about their workday with a supportive listener, while others need time for quiet reflection. Some people need entertainment, some need distraction, some need a drink, and some just need a hug.

Different recovery times

Richard Davidson, a neuroscientist at the University of Wisconsin, has spent decades studying the relationship between our emotions and various brain structures and neurological systems. In his book *The Emotional Life of Your Brain*, Davidson notes that people vary widely with regard to the speed with which we recover from adverse experiences. (Davidson calls this quality "resilience," but

I prefer "recovery time," as I use the former term more broadly when discussing our overall response to stress and challenges.) Davidson's research demonstrates that people with different recovery times even show different patterns of activity in their brains.

In practice, this means that someone who had an objectively horrible day at work may be in a good mood by the time they step out of the office, yet someone who encountered fewer challenges may still feel their impact well into the evening.

Different cultures

"Every relationship is a cross-cultural experience," according to John Gottman, an eminent psychologist at the University of Washington whose research has focused on marriage and committed relationships. In *Principia Amoris: The New Science of Love*, Gottman writes, even "if we come from the same country, the same part of the country, the same race, and the same religion, we come from . . . families that have defined meaning in very different ways. When we build a relationship together, we must decide on our own meanings."

But while couples may take the time to understand and evaluate their respective life goals and philosophies before embarking on a shared existence together, they rarely stop to think about the more mundane aspects of domestic life and what it means to build a cross-cultural relationship in those domains.

That's why spouses and partners may have significantly different interpretations and expectations about what it means to "come home" and how people are expected to interact on such an occasion.

How to Have a More Peaceful Reunion

So what can we do to fight less when we get home?

Recognize your differences

It's unrealistic and unhelpful for couples to expect that they'll automatically be in sync when they arrive home. Different needs, different recovery times, and different cultures all combine to make it *more* likely rather than not that couples will be *out* of sync when they first encounter each other at the end of the workday.

Identify your needs as individuals

Make time to talk as a couple about how your family comes together at the end of the day. Don't have this conversation when you first walk in the door—set some time aside when you and your partner are at your best. This may seem like a trivial issue to take so seriously, yet a consistent failure to recognize the importance of this encounter is precisely why so many couples find it so stressful. A little planning—and some candor about what you, your partner, and your kids need—goes a long way.

Regulate yourself

Practicing some degree of emotion management and self-monitoring can be particularly useful. We tend to approach our spouses and partners with the expectation that we can just be ourselves, without worrying about how we'll be perceived or our impact on them. And yet a consequence of this approach is that we take all the interpersonal skills that we work so hard to apply as leaders and managers, and we throw them out the window as we get close to home, just when they'd be most useful.

Adapted from content posted on hbr.org, April 12, 2016 (product #H02T76).

15

How to Help Your Partner Cope with Work Stress

by Rebecca Knight

Quick Takes

- Give your partner your undivided attention

- Be compassionate—not competitive

- Ask probing questions

- Consider the difference between sporadic and chronic stress

- Encourage your spouse to develop their support network

- Make your home a haven

Home is a sanctuary from work stress, right? Not always, especially if you or your spouse works from home (or work together outside of the home!). Even if you're able to shut down your laptop and your work worries at the end of your day, your spouse may have difficulty doing so—and that stress can rub off on you. How can you help your partner cope? What's the best thing to say when your partner starts complaining—and what should you *not* say? Is there a way to help them see things differently? And how can you set boundaries so that home can be a haven again?

What the Experts Say

Dealing with stress is a fact of working life. And when you're half of a dual-career couple, you have both your own stress to manage and your significant other's stress as well. But that's not necessarily a bad thing, according to Jennifer Petriglieri, assistant professor of organizational behavior at INSEAD. "Two careers can mean twice the stress, but it can also mean twice the empathy and understanding," she says. What's more, she adds, helping your partner learn to cope with stress helps you cope with it better, too. "When a couple is good at managing stress, it makes them [as individuals] more resilient." The key, says John Coleman, coauthor of the book *Passion & Purpose*, is to move away from the notion that "you're two individuals managing stress" and move toward the idea that "you're partners managing it together." Your goal, he adds, is to "become a constructive outlet" for your spouse. So, whether your significant other is stressing over a conflict with their boss, looming layoffs, or a crazy-making client, here are some pointers on how to help.

Listen

When your partner begins recounting their latest office irritation, many of us tend to "only half-listen" to them, Petriglieri says. "It's 7 p.m.—you're trying to make dinner and the kids are around—and so you nod and say, 'Uh-huh, uh-huh, uh-huh.'" But that's likely to leave your partner even more frustrated. Instead, she suggests, "give your partner your undivided attention." Listen and "really focus on what your partner is saying." Don't interrupt. "It's quite likely that your partner just needs to rant for three minutes and get something off their chest," she says. Don't offer advice—at least not yet, Coleman says. "You don't always need to be a problem solver," he adds. "Sometimes your partner just needs to be heard."

Offer support

It's critical to "show engagement in what your partner is saying," Coleman says. "Don't just look at them with a fixed stare." Instead, "say supportive things and use supportive language." Empathize and sympathize, but don't compare your stress to your spouse's. "When your partner starts complaining, don't say, 'Oh, you think your day was bad, listen to what I had to deal with!' It doesn't help anything." Stress endurance is not a competition. Still, it's not always easy to provide on-demand support and encouragement, and sometimes "you are not mentally ready to deal with your partner's problems," he says. If it's an inopportune time, Petriglieri suggests, offer to "follow up on the conversation later in the evening, the next day, or even on the weekend." The important thing is that you "leave the door open to further conversation."

Play career coach (judiciously)

"The benefit of having a spouse is that they know you as well as you know yourself"—maybe even a little better, Coleman says. "So if you get a sense that your partner is misreading a situation at work or heading in the wrong direction, you need to say something." He suggests "asking good questions that will broaden" your significant other's perspective. Try probing but nonthreatening lines of inquiry, such as, "'What makes you think that's the case?' Or, 'Is there a situation in which a different response would be warranted?' Sometimes you have to help your partner identify a blind spot," he says. Offer advice—but be gentle about it, Petriglieri says. She recommends saying something like, "'I have a suggestion on a path forward. Can I share it?' It takes the heat out of what you have to say."

Reflect

It's also important to be aware of the type of stress your partner is experiencing, according to Petriglieri. There are two kinds of work stress. "There's sporadic stress, which is the result of a bad meeting or a client project gone awry," and there's "chronic stress, which bubbles under the surface" for a prolonged period. Chronic stress, she says, is a signal that your significant other may "be in the wrong place." It's the "classic boiling-frog syndrome," she adds. To wit, you need to "notice your partner's attitude, mood, and patterns," and help them reflect on their career and professional path. "Ask, 'How are things going? Are you where you want to be? Are you satisfied?'" Granted, these questions are fodder "for a longer, meaningful conversation that's more appropriate for a night out or a long walk on the beach." But if your spouse is struggling, you need to be on top of it.

Encourage outside friendships and interests

Yet, "you cannot be the sole repository for your partner's stress," Coleman says. "Typically, partners are the ones we rely on the most. But relying on each other too much can sour a relationship." You and your partner should have lives outside of work and home. Give each other the freedom and space to pursue things you enjoy. Ideally, you'll each maintain an "outside support network" of "folks who can help you work through" professional challenges and serve as sounding boards and sources of counsel. Encourage your spouse to "keep up existing relationships" and "cultivate new friendships and connections," Petriglieri says. It might also be worthwhile to "encourage your partner to see a therapist or work with a career coach," she adds. "It could push [your spouse's] development forward." Bear in mind, though, the therapist or coach ought to be "a complement, not a substitute" for you.

Decompress together

Finally, cultivate "your home as a haven," Coleman says. This is easier said than done. The ubiquity of mobile phones and laptop computers and the 24/7 nature of work are big obstacles. That's why "you and your spouse need to practice good mobile device habits," he says. "There need to be times of day where you both put down your mobile phones; you need to draw a distinction of when a work device can be used at home." He also suggests helping your partner "develop a good end-of-work habit." It could be encouraging them to listen to an audiobook or music or just take a walk at the end of the workday. "You both need time to decompress."

Adapted from "How to Help Your Spouse Cope with Work Stress," on hbr.org, August 20, 2018 (product #H04I6P).

16

How to Support Your Partner During a Career Setback

by Deborah Grayson Riegel

Quick Takes

- Take a breath to counteract your body's natural fight-or-flight response to bad news

- Choose to maintain a positive mindset

- Remind your partner—and yourself—that you're on the same team

- Use language that validates and supports your partner

- Take good care of your own career

W hether it's a bad performance review or a layoff, a relocation or a reassignment, a missed promotion or a lost account, most of us have endured a career setback. Perhaps you experienced anxiety or depression as a result, or maybe you used the opportunity to reflect on your strengths and to take your time to figure out what's next.

Whatever you did to recover and bounce back from this setback, you probably had support. And if you were in a committed relationship, your partner was, hopefully, helpful to you in making it through this challenging time.

But what if the roles are now reversed? What if your partner experiences a career setback, and you're not sure what to say or do—as well as what *not* to say or do? You want to be empathetic, caring, and compassionate, of course. And you also realize that what just happened to them is also, in some way, happening to you.

How can you support your partner during a setback, while also taking care of your own career—and yourself? Here are five ways to help you both, including some sample language to start the conversation. Follow the tips in this order—or in whatever way works for your partner and your partnership. Use the scripts as a foundation or as inspiration to find words that feel like you.

1. Take a deep breath

When your partner shares their setback with you, you're likely to experience a "fight or flight" response. Your heart rate will increase, your breathing will get faster, and your blood pressure will rise. Such a reaction could trigger a decrease in rational thinking, decision-making, problem-solving, and collaborating. So before you speak, breathe.

Deep breathing is one of the best ways to manage this stress response. When you breathe deeply, your brain gets the message to relax—and then your brain shares that message with your body.

Deep breathing will allow your automatic threat responses to slow down, giving you more control over both your body and your mind—and hopefully your words.

(And, if you can, ask your partner to take a deep breath with you, too.)

2. Check your mindset

In her book, *Mindset: The New Psychology of Success*, Carol Dweck writes, "Mindsets are just beliefs. They're powerful beliefs, but they're just something in your mind, and you can change your mind."

Being able to change your mind (and your mindset) will enable you to have a helpful and supportive conversation about this setback. A key component of cognitive-behavioral therapy is the "cognitive triangle," which shows that our thoughts influence our feelings, which influence our behaviors.

If your current mindset is that this setback is a disaster, you're likely to feel anxious, angry, or helpless, which may lead you to act out or withdraw—none of which is helpful to your partner. And if your current belief is that you now have to be extra careful about not losing ground at your own job, you're likely to feel overwhelmed or even resentful. And behaviors that result from feeling overwhelmed or resentful at home—or at work—are unlikely to get you positive results.

I'm not suggesting that you deny or ignore those mindsets. They have value. They're alerting you to a threat. Trying to stuff them down or push them away won't work. What will? Choosing additional mindsets that are more helpful to bring to your conversations with your partner, and to your approach to your own work and career.

And mindsets, like emotions, can be contagious.

In 2008, as a result of the financial crisis, my then-nascent coaching and consulting business suffered a blow. Within a two-month time period, 100% of my work had been postponed or canceled.

I remember asking my husband, Michael, "Do I need to go out and find a real job?" to which he responded, "You have a real job. Just because you don't have clients right now doesn't mean you don't have a real job."

His mindset that my job was legitimate independent of workflow and income (at least temporarily) impacted my mindset in a positive, productive, and permanent way. How do I know? Because in March 2020, when my clients started postponing or canceling work as a result of the pandemic, I repeated his message, "I have a real job."

It goes both ways. My personal go-to mindset when Michael is experiencing a setback is this: "We've survived 100% of our setbacks together."

This belief leads me to feel calm, confident, and hopeful, and I am more likely to show up in the conversation as patient and optimistic. And when I speak with my husband in a patient and optimistic way, he is more likely to feel understood, cared for, and supported by me.

Some mindsets to consider include:

- "We will get through this."

- "I am safe."

- "This is temporary."

- "We're a great team."

And of course, you're welcome to borrow mine.

3. Don't think "breadwinner," think "breadsharer" (even if your earnings aren't truly "shared")

In chapter 3, Erin Reid writes that, for mixed-gender married couples, "different interpretations of the social status and financial value of their wives' careers provided men with different ways of approaching their own careers."

While husbands who saw themselves as "breadwinners" tended to be less focused on being flexible for their wive's careers, "breadsharers" demonstrated a commitment to be "professionally flexible to maximize their ability to respond to their wives' career opportunities and were hence uncommitted to any particular pathway and open to leaving their organization."

Regardless of gender, adopting a breadsharer approach when your partner has a career setback can help them feel like you're in it together, that you're a team, that you have shared responsibility and accountability for work and home, and that you are open to a range of options for what may come next.

When my career suffered that setback in 2008, I accepted a lucrative offer to teach executive communications at an MBA program in China. In order for me to take advantage of this opportunity across the globe, Michael and I discussed that he would need to take on the primary responsibility of caring for our then-7-year-old twins, while working his own full-time job. He agreed that he would do this to support me and our mutual financial and career goals. It was stressful for us both, yet significantly less so than it would have been if we hadn't viewed our financial and family responsibilities as shared.

And when Michael had his own career setback in a "last one hired, first one fired" situation, I started attending regular networking events to meet connections for both of us. I also suggested that he use the gap time to get credentialed as a coach, since I believed it to be a useful skill set for whatever his next role would be. (Fast-forward six years, and he is now a full-time executive coach!)

Taking a breadsharer approach may also mean putting one of your own goals on hold, temporarily, while you and your partner focus on the other's. So, for example, if you were planning to leave your job to look for a new opportunity, but now you're the primary source of income and benefits, name it—but without shame, blame, or guilt. Rather than saying, "So I guess it looks like I'm not going to be leaving my go-nowhere job anytime soon, huh?" (even if you're really feeling it), try "I'm going to put my job search on hold for now. I'm disappointed, of course. And once we get you back on track, I'll pick it back up. How does that sound?"

4. Choose helpful language

One of the core principles of Appreciative Inquiry, a strengths-based approach to leadership development and organizational change that I use with my clients, is that "words create worlds." Our language shapes the way we experience reality. When your partner is experiencing a career setback, choose language that supports them and their experience, rather than exacerbates or negates them.

Exacerbating language often blames, shames, or adds pressure. This can sound like:

- "How could you let this happen?"

- "I can't deal with this right now!"

- "What are we supposed to do?"

- "This is your problem, not mine."

- "Again?"

Those are phrases that ignite the emotional heat for your partner, and between you and your partner. Contrast that with language that tries to ignore or even smother the emotional impact of a setback. If your partner is negative, you might be tempted to shift their focus to something more positive. But if they're not ready, your attempts to lift the mood may be experienced as lacking empathy.

Secure Bases and Loving Kicks: A Conversation with Jennifer Petriglieri

Women at Work spoke with Jennifer Petriglieri, a professor at INSEAD, who studied 50 dual-career, highly educated opposite-sex couples from countries around the world. We asked her to tell us more about her research and how the psychological support we get at home shapes our identities at work. She advises partners to serve as a secure base for each other but also to deliver loving kicks as they support each other in work and in life.

SARAH GREEN CARMICHAEL: *One of the findings from your study is that thriving couples experienced each other as a secure base. What is a secure base?*

JENNIFER PETRIGLIERI: The support we often initially crave, and we think about from our partners, is very much the tea-and-sympathy support. When we face a setback in our careers, like not getting that promotion or not getting the job we wanted, our immediate reaction is to think, I want a little bit of mollycoddling. I want someone who's going to take my side, tell me I'm great, and sort of cocoon me.

But we find that the support that really matters is that, plus a push out. A push away from that security blanket

(continued)

Secure Bases and Loving Kicks:
A Conversation with Jennifer Petriglieri

by saying something like, "Well, what are you going to do about that? How are you going to change this? How are you going to make it the world you want it to be?"

What's counterintuitive about that is, instead of keeping our partners very close, we're actually pushing them away from the relationship. Obviously in a loving way. And we're not interfering with that exploration. We're not saying, "Have you done XYZ? Have you followed up?" We're really giving our partners the independence to go and explore and grow and develop in the way they need to. And sometimes this might not feel very nice. We all want that love and sympathy and the cuddles. And sometimes when we're feeling vulnerable and wobbly, we don't really want to be pushed back out into the world. But we know from many decades of studies on psychological development that this is how we thrive. This is how we develop and grow: by picking ourselves up and going back out there and trying again and exploring.

NICOLE TORRES: *Can you give us an example of what being a secure base looks like from your own experience?*

JP: I'll give an example, which might be familiar to many couples. I had two children relatively close together; they were 16 months apart. It was a period that was very busy for me: I was doing my PhD; we had two under-twos. Anyone who's ever had two under twos knows how crazy that can be, and how wonderful it is, but it is crazy. I went through a period of thinking, I just cannot keep this up. There is no way I can keep my career going and be the kind of mother I want to be.

At times like that, many women get the message from their partners, and from other people around them: Don't worry. Take some time out. It'll be fine. But we know that that's a total career killer, how hard it is for women to get back in the game. When this happened to me, my husband said, "There is no way you are giving up your career. I'm not going to let you. You will regret it."

Now, at that time, did I like what he said? No. But was he right? Absolutely. If he hadn't given me that kick to carry on, my career would not be where it is today.

So many women don't get that loving kick and they opt out. They get the tea and sympathy. And they get support, but they don't get that little extra push that would really make the difference in their careers.

Excerpted from "Couples That Work: An Interview with Jennifer Petriglieri," *Women at Work* podcast, season 1, episode 2, February 1, 2018.

These are some negating phrases that can be categorized as "toxic positivity":

- "Everything happens for a reason."

- "You'll bounce back—you always do."

- "Think positive!"

- "There are so many people who have it worse than you."

- "What doesn't kill us makes us stronger."

So, you might be asking yourself, "What *can* I say?"

You can say anything you want, of course, but you will be most helpful if you use language that meets your partner where they are now, rather than trying to shock them into action or get them to feel something that makes *you* more comfortable.

Try saying:

- "Thank you for talking to me about this."

- "I know this is hard."

- "I am here to support you through this."

- "What can I take off your plate?"

- "Let's make a plan."

- "I've been through something like this. And while I don't want to make this about me, I am open to sharing my experience with you if and when it would be helpful."

- "How can I help?"

You may also want to negotiate language around sensitive issues of privacy. While you might want to confide in your colleague that your partner lost a big client, your partner may not want you to share it yet—or at all. Consider asking your partner, "Who can we share this with?," "What parts do we want to share—and what don't we want to share?," and "When can we revisit when we share this with others?"

Also advocate for your own needs. If you want to let someone close to you know what's happening—because you need their help with networking, an accommodation to your schedule, or some emotional support—share this with your partner. It's better to have this conversation up front than to have secrets.

5. Take care of your career, and yourself

You might find that your partner can't fully be there for you right now. They may be feeling overwhelmed, depressed, or stuck. Maybe you suggested they meet with a career coach (so that you can be their partner, not their coach), and they've declined. Or maybe they'd agreed to accompany you to your annual holiday party, and they're just not in the mood.

That has an impact on you. Negative emotions are contagious, and your partner's stress is likely to make you feel stressed, too. And while you might feel distracted or overwhelmed, you don't want to let your stress impact the quality of your own work. Honor your commitments and responsibilities, deliver excellent work, and do what it takes to continue to be seen as a reliable contributor and leader.

Make sure that you also take care of yourself emotionally, physically, financially, spiritually, and more—even if your partner doesn't want any part of it. This can range from going for a walk, attending religious services, or calling a financial planner to picking up an old hobby or a new skill or seeing a mental health professional for yourself.

In order for you to be there for your partner during a career setback, you need to be there for yourself, too. That way, when your partner is ready, willing, and able to be a part of healing the past and preparing for the future, you have the strength, the reserves, and the desire to be a part of that conversation as well.

Epilogue

The Greatest Adventure

17

Teamwork Makes the Dream Work

Contributed by 19 HBR readers

Quick Takes

- Define balance for yourselves—it can be a percentage or taking turns

- Create and share a calendar system that works for everyone, even your kids

- Talk about your career goals to help your family understand the impact of your time away from them

- Identify a metaphor to help you remember there will be highs and lows and periods of busy and calm (waves, seasons, and the like)

- Know that life will not go according to plan, so stay flexible

Editor's Note: When you're part of a two-career family, can you each chase your dreams, raise good citizens, make time for hobbies and health, and nourish your relationship well enough that you still like each other when your nest is empty and you're in the final acts of your careers?

We reached out to working parents on HBR's LinkedIn Discussion Group and asked them to share their hacks, highlights, and words of wisdom for managing two careers while raising a family. Great stories and suggestions poured in from around the globe, from all types of couples, with kids of all ages. We've collected some of our favorites here.

Balance doesn't always mean 50/50

Early in my career I asked a *Fortune* 500 executive whom I aspired to be like (powerhouse career and growing family) how she did it—balanced work and life aspirations successfully. She told me it was hard work but not necessarily a balance in the way I was describing. Balance for her didn't mean a 50/50 split or striving for 50/50 but often looked like 80/20. Sometimes family got the 80% and work 20%; other times work got 80% and home 20%.

I've lived by those words for the last 10 years. It has made a world of difference to me, empowered me to feel confident in what I give to my colleagues and to my husband and kids, regardless of which is getting 80%, as long as the pendulum swings back and forth.

—KATIE T., mom of three, USA

Ride the wave

Get comfortable being uncomfortable, and lower your personal expectations of what "good" looks like. Recognise you are always just riding a wave (in any area of your life) with a high and low tide that peaks differently each time; a house in disarray is simply a low tide. Mess in moments of chaos is best dealt with laughter rather than anxiety and stress.

—GILLIAN M., mother of three, Australia

Engage your kids in your work narrative

Involve your kids in the stories pertaining to your work. Identify the main "characters" in your work narrative—the folks they hear about most. Sharing the good and the bad of what happens at work can be a tool to teach them life lessons. It's an easy way to help your kids feel involved in a part of your life that they sometimes think they're "competing" with.

—MAHZARINE J., mother of two, India

It doesn't get easier; it's just different

We raised our kids with one of us working full-time (and doing an OU degree) and the other working shifts. Now we're juggling both needing the study all day, figuring out who does the work lifts for our teenager, and wondering if anyone fed the cat today. It doesn't let up; it just changes.

—**ELIZABETH B.**, mum of two, UK

Take turns taking risks

We are in this journey with a strategy that we believe might work. While I am providing business-as-usual stability, my wife has taken the risks of a startup-innovation journey. Eventually, I will have a turn to take a risk once her journey becomes business-as-usual.

—**NITIN C.**, father of two, India

Redefine success

With a 2.5-year-old and a 3-month-old, and both my husband and I working from home, success sometimes feels like just getting through the day. Our most special moments occur around the dinner table—a sacred time for us all to be together. We often each work late into the night afterward, but that two-hour evening window with our family is nonnegotiable. We talk about successes and failures of the day, why we're proud of each other, and our problems. After dinner, we often have a dance party while doing the dishes together before bath time. It's a lot different than the romance we shared before we become parents, but in many ways it's even better.

—**COLLEEN K.**, mother of two, USA

Have everyone pitch in

I started my PhD after having two kids with no family support except my spouse, who also started a new job at that time. I failed to try to manage the house by myself. I struggled a lot.

The thing that worked for us is that we all assumed responsibilities. We considered everyone as equal partners in running the family—even my 5-year-old. We identified the critical tasks that have to be completed by the end of the day. Everyone completes the tasks that they are good at. And we cover each other when the other person is busy with something else.

—**NILA D.**, mother of two, Canada

Set a plan and have faith

My husband and I both have demanding careers. Our children are involved in extracurricular activities, including Amateur Athletic Union (AAU) sports teams that require travel.

For us, it all started with a conversation premarriage where we agreed on what we wanted and what we will do . . . it works because we hold steady to those agreements and respect what's important to the other. We pitch in together where we can and lead in the space where we are each stronger. We have high bars for our children, and they make us proud every day.

—**JUDIA J.**, mother of three, USA

Take storytime on the road

As a female executive, it's hard to travel with young children at home. My children are now grown, but I share this story with younger female colleagues, clients, and friends.

Weekends for my family included trips to the bookstore to purchase "mommy's travel books." We would get two copies of children's books the kids picked out—one for them and one for me to take with me. While I was away, I would call home to read to my children. This allowed me time with my family, no matter where I was. This small gesture selfishly took away some of the "mommy guilt" that we all have. More importantly, the kids' excitement at having me read to them at night, rather than awful thoughts that "Mom is not here," is something I cherish. (And, yes, it also gave my husband a well-deserved break in the evening!)

—**BETH F.**, mother of two, USA

Share your calendar—and your goals

I've found that managing our calendar together helps us stay on track. We circle events or appointments that cannot be moved or changed. Use this tag wisely or you'll lose its value. Unless unavoidable, all dates/appointments are tentative until you've discussed them with your partner (and that includes playdates, sleepovers, travel out of town, routine doctor visits, etc.).

We also talk about our long-term goals. Vocalize your career ambitions with each other so you can each appreciate the effort and sacrifices required. If your children are old enough, share your goals with them too. It can help them make sense of the implications.

—**MICHAEL W.**, father of two, USA

Know you will drop the ball

Make peace with the fact that there is a juggle, and a ball or three will be dropped more often than not—and that it is OK. Don't judge yourself, your partner, or your kids too harshly when that happens. Admit that it happened, and aim to get to it when you can.

—**ARTHI R.**, mum of one, South Africa

Communication and care make everything work

My husband and I have learned that there will be times when one spouse's professional goals require them to devote more resources to the office, and those times will require the other parent to flex more at home. It was key for us to identify those shifts, communicate openly about them, and ultimately both agree on the timeline/compromises needed to avoid resentment.

I'll also add that having affordable and high-quality childcare is the only way we're able to be a two-career family. I recognize that in this country, we're very fortunate to have access to that. Many, many people do not, and women disproportionately bear that burden.

—**LAUREN A.,** mother of one, USA

Enjoy this busy season

We are a blended family and are like a girl-only version of the *Brady Bunch*. We each have three girls, so a total of six kids—five of them are teens. For us the main "survival tools" are communication and organization. We have our kids take ownership of and communicate their events, things they need, sports schedules, when they'll need rides, etc. ahead of time. With that information, my husband and I decide how we'll conquer and divide.

We remind each other to not sweat the small stuff, laugh, and enjoy this busy season in our lives where we get to raise these amazing kids we so love, as it will be over before we know it.

—**HEIDI B.**, mother of three and stepmother of three, USA

Turn challenges into opportunities

My husband is a civil servant with the government, in Indian Railways. He would get transferred every three years—sometimes sooner! We were frequently packing and setting up a new house in a new location . . . with new schools, new environment, new friends! I worked at the university and at corporations, and I would resign as soon as my husband's transfer orders came. It somehow felt right to move with the family and especially with two boys in their formative years. We adopted a mindset that from all of these transitions we were gaining "high adaptability." I would tell my sons that "frequent change is an opportunity for you. You will be able to confront most situations in life as a result of moving so often."

—**DR. ANJALI N.**, mother of two, India

Make time for individual interests

We struggled for a while with being a two-career family. Being parents to three kids, with two demanding jobs (and some travel), forced us to reevaluate a lot. What saved us was finding passions outside of work and giving each other time at nights and on weekends. My husband is a golfer, and I got back into painting. I learned oil painting (a dream of mine since I was little) and am launching a collection later this year. We block time for what we love and support each other.

—**MEGAN S.,** mother of three, USA

Prioritize date nights

For our family, one thing that worked was for my husband and I to go out on a date once a week, just to get away from chaos and have time together. We have been practicing weekly dating for over 20 years. In Hong Kong, we had a live-in domestic helper. So we let her take care of our son while we went out for a simple dinner. It was NOT fine dining or fancy meals. We just paid attention to one another and did some grocery shopping after. Our son got used to it and knew that his parents had their special evening without him.

—**KARA C.,** mother of one, Hong Kong

Be a team

Teamwork makes the dream work. As cheesy as that sounds, we are a team and operate as such. We take turns taking the kids to appointments, sports, sick days. We talk often about what we need as far as support. We give each other grace when one of us needs a break. We are able to balance who needs to work late or travel, and who can be the mystery reader for first grade.

—**SUSAN B.**, mother of two, USA

The journey is long, with many stages

What helps me is to remember that marriage is a journey with many stages, as is parenthood. Even though you work separate careers, and one may be further along than the other, remember that you are on the same team. Celebrate where each of you are at each stage.

Remember that every parent is part of the parent tribe and we are all in different stages and careers, with different resources. Whenever possible, make new friends and help one another and let others help you. I will always be indebted to the friend who came over to help with our child, and even help clean up when we had no family or other resources. And I have been glad to reciprocate for many other families!

Have empathy and don't judge yourself or others, nor be envious. The journey is long, and each step builds character.

Finally, make sure to eat ice cream together, sing karaoke, and laugh at the top of your lungs together, at least once a week.

—**CAT S.**, mother of one extraordinary kid, USA

Let love rule

A wise coach advised me to:

- Define my and my spouse's nonnegotiables and work around that (no pun intended!) so we can stay united. Work should follow what each of us believes is truly essential to living.

- Be respectful—of preferences, of circumstances, of missed expectations, of your own health, of your kids who are blooming into their uniqueness, and most of all, the person you married.

- In all things, try to find LOVE. I suppose that includes loving the work you do, the family by your side, and the gift of life!

—**JO-ANNE C.,** mom of two, Philippines

NOTES

Chapter 1

1. "Raising Kids and Running a Household: How Working Parents Share the Load," Pew Research Center, November 4, 2015, https://www.pewsocialtrends.org/2015/11/04/raising-kids-and-running-a-household-how-working-parents-share-the-load/.

2. I studied 113 dual-career couples ranging in age from 26 to 63, with an even distribution among age groups. The majority of couples—76—were in their first significant partnership. Participants in the study came from 32 countries on four continents, and their ethnic and religious backgrounds reflected this diversity. At the time of the study, roughly 35% resided in North America, 40% in Europe, and 25% in the rest of the world. In 68 of the couples at least one partner had children. Eleven of the couples identified as gay, and the rest as straight. Just under 60% of the participants were pursuing careers in the corporate world. The others were spread roughly equally among the professions (such as medicine, law, and academia), entrepreneurship, government, and the nonprofit sector.

Chapter 2

1. Gang Wang, In-Sue Oh, Stephen H. Courtright, and Amy E. Colbert, "Transformational Leadership and Performance Across Criteria and Levels: A Meta-Analytic Review of 25 Years of Research," *Group & Organization Management* 36, no. 2 (2011): 223–270.

2. Laura Parks-Leduc, Gilad Feldman, and Anat Bardi, "Personality Traits and Personal Values: A Meta-Analysis," *Personality and Social Psychology Review* 19, no. 1 (2015): 3–29.

3. David A. Kenny and Linda K. Acitelli, "Accuracy and Bias in the Perception of the Partner in a Close Relationship," *Journal of Personality and Social Psychology* 80, no 3 (2001): 439–448.

Chapter 3

1. E. M. Reid, "Straying from Breadwinning: Status and Money in Men's Interpretations of Their Wives' Work Arrangements," *Gender, Work, and Organization* 25, no. 6 (2018): 718–733.

Chapter 5

1. Sulin Ba and Lei Wang, "Digital Health Communities: The Effect of Their Motivation Mechanisms," *Decision Support Systems* 55, no. 4 (2013): 941–947.

2. Emma E. A. Cohen et al., "Rowers' High: Behavioural Synchrony Is Correlated with Elevated Pain Thresholds," *Biology Letters* 6, no. 1 (2009).

3. Leo Babauta, "Review Your Goals Weekly," Zen Habits, n.d., https://zenhabits.net/review-your-goals-weekly/; Gina Trapani, "How to Write To-Do Lists That Work," *Harvard Business Review*, January 13, 2009.

4. Noah J. Goldstein, Steve J. Martin, and Robert B. Cialdini, *Yes! 50 Scientifically Proven Ways to Be Persuasive* (New York: Free Press, 2008).

Chapter 6

1. Michael R. Frone, Marcia Russell, and M. Lynne Cooper, "Prevalence of Work-Family Conflict: Are Work and Family Boundaries Asymmetrically Permeable?" *Journal of Organizational Behavior* 13, no. 7 (1992): 723–729.

2. Penny Edgell Becker and Phyllis Moen, "Scaling Back: Dual-Earner Couples' Work-Family Strategies," *Journal of Marriage and Family* 61, no. 4 (1999): 995–1007.

3. Robin J. Ely, Pamela Stone, and Colleen Ammerman, "Rethink What You 'Know' About High-Achieving Women," *Harvard Business Review*, December 2014.

Chapter 8

1. Mojca Filipič Sterle et al., "Expatriate Family Adjustment: An Overview of Empirical Evidence on Challenges and Resources," *Frontiers in Psychology* 9 (2018): 1207.

Chapter 9

1. PwC and the Cranfield School of Management, "Measuring the Value of International Assignments," 2006, https://www.pwc.fi/fi/palvelut/tiedostot/pwc_measuring_the_value.pdf.

2. Brookfield Global Relocation Services, "2016 Global Mobility Trends," http://globalmobilitytrends.bgrs.com/.

Chapter 12

1. Samuel S. Monfort, Hannah E. Stroup, and Christian E. Waugh, "The Impact of Anticipating Positive Events on Responses to Stress," *Journal of Experimental Social Psychology* 58 (2015): 11–22.

Chapter 13

1. Amie M. Gordon, Belinda Carrillo, and Christopher M. Barnes, "Sleep and Social Relationships in Healthy Populations: A Systematic Review," *Sleep Medicine Reviews* 57 (2021): 101428.

2. Amie M. Gordon and Serena Chen, "The Role of Sleep in Interpersonal Conflict: Do Sleepless Nights Mean Worse Fights?" *Social Psychological and Personality Science* 5, no. 2 (2014): 168–175.

3. Angela M. Hicks and Lisa M. Diamond, "Don't Go to Bed Angry: Attachment, Conflict, and Affective and Physiological Reactivity," *Personal Relationships* 18 (2011): 266–284.

4. Mona El-Sheikh, Joseph A. Buckhalt, Jacquelyn Mize, and Christine Acebo, "Marital Conflict and Disruption of Children's Sleep," *Child Development* 77 (2006): 31–43; Chrystyna D. Kouros and Mona El-Sheikh, "Within-Family Relations in Objective Sleep Duration, Quality, and Schedule," *Child Development* 88 (2017): 1983–2000.

5. Annie Bernier, Marie-Ève Bélanger, Stéphanie Bordeleau, and Julie Carrier, "Mothers, Fathers, and Toddlers: Parental Psychosocial Functioning as a Context for Young Children's Sleep," *Developmental Psychology* 49, no. 7 (2013): 1375–1384.

6. Lucy S. King et al., "Mothers' Postpartum Sleep Disturbance Is Associated with the Ability to Sustain Sensitivity Toward Infants," *Sleep Medicine* 65 (2020): 74–83.

7. Teresa A. Lillis et al., "Sleep Quality Buffers the Effects of Negative Social Interactions on Maternal Mood in the 3–6 Month Postpartum Period: A Daily Diary Study," *Journal of Behavioral Medicine* 41 (2018) 733–746; Sheila W. McDonald, Heather L. Kehler, and Suzanne C. Tough, "Protective Factors for Child Development at Age 2 in the Presence of Poor Maternal Mental Health: Results from the All Our Babies (AOB) Pregnancy Cohort," *BMJ Open* 6 (2016): https://doi:10.1136/bmjopen-2016-012096.

8. Christopher M. Barnes and Nathaniel F. Watson, "Why Healthy Sleep Is Good for Business," *Sleep Medicine Reviews* 47 (2019): 112–118.

9. CDC, "How Much Sleep Do I Need?" https://www.cdc.gov/sleep/about_sleep/how_much_sleep.html.

10. M. R. Haley and Laurie A. Miller, "Correlates of Flexible Working Arrangements, Stress, and Sleep Difficulties in the US Workforce: Does the Flexibility of the Flexibility Matter?," *Empirical Economics* 48 (2015): 1395–1418.

ABOUT THE CONTRIBUTORS

DAISY DOWLING, SERIES EDITOR, is the founder and CEO of Workparent, the executive coaching and training firm, and the author of *Workparent: The Complete Guide to Succeeding on the Job, Staying True to Yourself, and Raising Happy Kids* (Harvard Business Review Press, 2021). She is a full-time working parent to two young children. She can be reached at www.workparent.com.

CHRISTOPHER M. BARNES is a professor of organizational behavior at the University of Washington's Foster School of Business. He worked in the Fatigue Countermeasures branch of the Air Force Research Laboratory before pursuing his PhD in organizational behavior at Michigan State University and has kept sleep as his primary research interest. He has twin toddlers and a preschooler and thus understands sleep deprivation from an experiential perspective as well.

ED BATISTA is an executive coach and lecturer at the Stanford Graduate School of Business. He writes regularly on issues related to coaching and professional development at edbatista.com. And he tweets about living on a farm and his dog Buster @edbatista.

RUSSELL CLAYTON is a faculty member in the Muma College of Business at the University of South Florida. He also serves as a well-being coach for employees who seek to have fruitful professional and personal lives. Russell is a husband and the father of two wonderful daughters and can often be found with his family at Disney World or at one of Florida's many sunny beaches. Connect with him at www.russellclayton.net.

JACKIE COLEMAN is a former marriage counselor and has recently worked on education programs for the state of Georgia and as a classroom teacher for young children.

JOHN COLEMAN is a business executive and the author of *The HBR Guide to Crafting Your Purpose* (Harvard Business Review Press, 2021). Jackie and John Coleman are married and have four young children.

STEWART D. FRIEDMAN, an organizational psychologist at the Wharton School, is the author of three Harvard Business Review Press books—*Parents Who Lead* (2020), *Leading the Life You Want* (2014), and *Total Leadership* (2008). He founded the Wharton Leadership Program, the Wharton Work/Life Integration Project, and Total Leadership, a management consulting and training company. His three grown children work in education. He hopes his three grandchildren will help us heal our broken world.

AMIE M. GORDON is an assistant professor of psychology at the University of Michigan, Ann Arbor, where she directs the Well-being, Health, and Interpersonal Relationships Lab (WHIRL). She received her PhD in social-personality psychology from the University of California, Berkeley. As a working mother who functions best on nine hours of sleep, much of her research on sleep and its effects on relationships has been inspired by her own nights of sleep deprivation and that desire to get one more thing done before she goes to bed.

REBECCA KNIGHT is a freelance journalist in Boston whose work has been published in the *New York Times*, *USA Today*, and the *Financial Times*. She is the mom of two tweenage daughters.

DANIELLE LINDEMANN is a sociologist at Lehigh University and the author of *Commuter Spouses*. She has two daughters and is an expert at turning tiny clothes right side out.

JENNIFER PETRIGLIERI is an associate professor of organizational behavior at INSEAD and the author of *Couples That Work* (Harvard Business Review Press, 2019).

She is the mum of Pietro (11) and Arianna (10), and together they enjoy growing vegetables, jumping on their trampoline, and going for long bike rides.

ERIN REID is an associate professor of human resources and management at McMaster University's DeGroote School of Business and holds a PhD in organizational behavior and sociology from Harvard University. Her three children, who are in daycare, elementary school, and middle school, keep her busy with soccer practices, Lego cleanup, and ice cream dates.

DEBORAH GRAYSON RIEGEL is a leadership consultant, keynote speaker, and an executive coach. She has taught for Wharton Business School, Columbia Business School, and Duke Corporate Education. She is the author of *Overcoming Overthinking*. Her husband Michael is also an executive coach, and their college-age twins, Jake and Sophie, catch their parents trying to coach them all the time.

ELIZABETH GRACE SAUNDERS is a time management coach and the founder of Real Life E Time Coaching & Speaking. She is the author of *How to Invest Your Time Like Money* and *Divine Time Management*. Find out more at www.RealLifeE.com. As a godmother and foster mom, she's refined the art of getting kids to church on time, tiring them out so much they sleep through the night, and having so much fun with them they talk about it for weeks.

AMY JEN SU is a cofounder and managing partner of Paravis Partners, a premier executive coaching and leadership development firm. For the past two decades, she has coached CEOs, executives, and rising stars in organizations. She is the author of *The Leader You Want to Be* (Harvard Business Review Press, 2019) and coauthor, with Muriel Maignan Wilkins, of *Own the Room* (Harvard Business Review Press, 2013). Amy is also a full-time working parent with a teenage son who is currently in high school. She spends nonwork time helping him practice driving to get his license, engaging in college prep, and talking about the highs and lows of navigating being a teenager.

MONIQUE VALCOUR is an executive coach, keynote speaker, and management professor. She helps clients create and sustain fulfilling and high-performance jobs, careers, workplaces, and lives. Her greatest joy in life is talking and laughing with her husband and two adult daughters. Contact her at www.moniquevalcour.com.

KATIA VLACHOS is a certified Co-Active coach and the author of *A Great Move: Surviving and Thriving in*

Your Expat Assignment. A researcher by training with a PhD in policy analysis from the RAND Corporation, Katia helps her globally mobile clients engage with life's transitions and build a thriving life abroad. She's the mother of two teens and a 10-year-old who's already acting like one.

ALYSSA F. WESTRING is an organizational psychologist and Vincent de Paul Professor of Management at DePaul University's Driehaus College of Business. She is a co-author of *Parents Who Lead* (Harvard Business Review Press, 2020), director of research at Total Leadership, and a certified diversity professional. She has two school-aged children and lives happily car-free on the South Side of Chicago. Follow her on Twitter @alyssawestring.

ANIA WIECKOWSKI is an executive editor at *Harvard Business Review.* She loves spending weekend time with her young goddaughter and a handful of other honorary nieces and nephews.

INDEX

Find fulfillment at home and at work with the HBR Working Parents Series

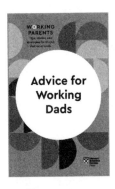

Advice for Working Dads

Advice for Working Moms

Communicate Better with Everyone

Getting It All Done

Managing Your Career

Taking Care of Yourself

FOR MORE, VISIT **HBR.ORG/BOOKS**

An all-in-one resource for every working parent.

If you enjoyed this book and want more guidance on working parenthood, turn to *Workparent: The Complete Guide to Succeeding on the Job, Staying True to Yourself, and Raising Happy Kids*. Written by Daisy Dowling, a top executive coach, talent expert, and working mom, *Workparent* provides all the advice and assurance you'll need to combine children and career in your own, authentic way.

AVAILABLE IN PAPERBACK
OR EBOOK FORMAT.

---

store.hbr.org

Buy for your team, clients, or event.
Visit hbr.org/bulksales for quantity discount rates.